How to Accept the Gift of Eternal Life

Larry Moench Davis

Copyright © 2002
Larry Moench Davis
http://www.larrymoenchdavis.com
Published by Zion's Publishing Company

ISBN 0-9670193-5-4
Library of Congress Control Number: 2002103094

All rights reserved.

No portion of this publication may be reproduced, stored in a retrieval system, or transmitted in any form whatsoever, whether electronic, mechanical, photocopying, recording, or by any other means except for brief quotations in printed reviews, without the prior written permission from Zion's Publishing Company, P.O. Box 150008, Ogden, Utah 84415.

Table of Contents

Introduction 4

Chapter

   1   The Plan.. 7

   2   Life After Death... 19

   3   The First Requirement to Qualify
       for Eternal Life 55

   4   The Second Requirement to Qualify
       for Eternal Life 68

   5   The Third Requirement to Qualify
       for Eternal Life 105

   6   The Fourth Requirement to Qualify
       for Eternal Life 121

   7   The Fifth Requirement to Qualify
       for Eternal Life 151

Introduction

An interesting story is told about an eagle and a salesman. The salesman came to a small farm house on the outskirts of town. Observing the farmer out tending to some chores in front of the house, the salesman asked if he could obtain lodging for the night. The farmer graciously invited the salesman to stay as long as he wanted.

The next morning, to show his appreciation for the hospitality, the salesman helped the farmer with his morning chores. While feeding the chickens, the salesman noticed that in one corner of the yard, with some other chickens was a golden eagle. Fearing the eagle would harm the chickens, the salesman called to the farmer. Quickly, the farmer ran to the chicken yard, but when he discovered the cause of the ruckus, he just laughed.

He then told the salesman that two years before, one of

his sons had found an egg in a nest high up on the cliffs behind his home. The son had returned to the farm with the egg and had placed it under one of the brooding hens to see what would happen. Eventually, the egg hatched and a baby eagle was raised by the mother hen as a chicken. The eagle, being raised with chickens, acted as a chicken.

After hearing the story, the salesman told the farmer that it made little difference how the eagle was raised; it was still an eagle. The farmer again laughed and said, "No, it's a chicken. Why, it can't even fly."

To find out, the salesman picked up the eagle and tried to get it to fly, but it simple fluttered to the earth and continued to peck the ground in search of food. The farmer just chuckled and told the salesman it was no use, the bird would never fly.

Later that day, as the salesman was out making his rounds, he kept thinking of how the eagle was wasting its life. Since the salesman did not finish his work that day. He received permission to stay another night.

Just before dark, the salesman again found himself in the chicken yard trying to coax the eagle into the air, but to no avail. Early the next morning, as the sun peeked above the rolling hills, the salesman picked up the eagle for one last try. Holding the magnificent bird high above his head, he began running toward the rising sun. Suddenly he could feel the claws slowly begin to release their grip to his arm; the giant wings began to spread, mechanically beating the air with evenly measured strokes. Gracefully, the giant bird lifted into the air, descended slightly, then picking up speed, lifted higher and higher until it became lost in the early morning haze. "Now," thought the salesman, "you are no longer a chicken, but a golden eagle, king of the air."

William Wordsworth wrote: "Our birth is but a sleep and a forgetting; the Soul that rises with us, our life's Star, hath elsewhere had its setting and cometh from afar: not in entire forgetfulness, and not in utter nakedness, but trailing clouds of glory do we come from God, who is our home."

Who are we? Where did we come from? Why are we here? Could it be that, like the eagle, we too have a misconception as to who we really are and what our purpose of existence is all about?

This book is written to provide answers to these questions.

1

The Plan

Originally, this book was part of a single large volume composed of two parts. Part 1 presented information to help an individual understand the meaning of life as outlined in the Holy Bible. This information was published in my book called *Understanding the Gift of Mortal Life*. During Biblical times the prophets of both the Old and New testaments used the terms "immortality" and "eternal life" to describe our state of being after we die.

At first glance it appears that these terms are just different ways to describe the ability to live forever. However, as one comes to understand more details of the great plan, it becomes apparent that the prophets understood these terms to have different meanings. The term *immortality* denotes the ability to live forever. However, the term *eternal life* describe an incredible, fantastic gift. This gift is an idyllic quality of life (as in Shangri-la) that some will receive as a reward for righteous living. It involves the inheritance of great power, authority, and the opportunity to participate in future creations.

Since a gift cannot be imparted to an individual unless that person performs some physical action to accept the gift, the gift of eternal life also requires that we qualify ourselves so we can be worthy to accept this gift.

God has told us what we must do, and this information is recorded in both the Old and New Testaments. What are the requirements? Part 2 of the original manuscript described these requirements but was not lengthy enough to do justice to them. The only answer was to make Part 2 the subject of a separate book, and *How to Accept the Gift of Eternal Life* is the result. Before we can discuss the requirements God would have us fulfill to make ourselves worthy to receive the gift of eternal life, it is necessary to review some of the major ingredients of God's great plan as outlined in *Understanding the Gift of Mortal Life*.

One reason for starting with the Old Testament was to point out that if the great plan of God was detailed in that book, (and the God of the Old Testament is the same God of the New Testament), then the same plan should be found in the New Testament but amplified in greater detail, because more knowledge was given by God. I selected the King James version of the Bible for two reasons: first, because the first five books are very similar to the Tanach, which is the Jewish Bible; second, because of its universal acceptance by most Christian denominations. This is important, because whether one believes in only the Old Testament or only the New Testament, the great plan of God is the same for all believers, and the requirements to receive the gift of eternal life are the same for everyone.

During our search, the information found in the Old and New Testaments taught the following basic concepts (scriptural support is documented in the book *Understanding the Gift of Mortal Life*):

From this book we learned that God does exist, that at least seventy-seven people actually saw God and walked and talked with Him. He first appeared to Adam and Eve. Finally, God was seen by Jacob, Moses, Aaron, Nadab, Abihu, and seventy of the elders of Israel.

If We Were to See God, What Would He Look like?

The Old Testament taught that if we were to see God, He would look very much like we do, with a head, face, body, arms, hands, and feet.

What Is the True Character and Personality of God?

The scriptures of the Old Testament testified that God's work is perfect. He is just and fair in all things. He always speaks the truth, and wickedness is an abomination to His lips. He delights in showing mercy and does not retain His anger forever. He has perfect knowledge of all things, is all-powerful, and feels emotions.

What Is Our Relationship to God?

The Old Testament prophet Malachi taught that God loves us and is concerned about our welfare, because He is the father of the spirits of all mankind. Since we are His spirit sons and daughters, it means we are all spirit brothers and sisters to each other.

Where Did We Come From?

We learned from the Old Testament that our spirits were created by God in heaven before we ever came to earth and that our spirits will return to the presence of God when we die. We had existed as spirits in heaven for some time before the foundations of this earth were even laid.

Why Did God Send Us to Earth?

The Old Testament scriptures taught that, since God is the father of our spirit being, He loves us and wants us to have the opportunity to develop our character attributes to be like His, perfect in all things, such as truth, integrity, honesty, wisdom, etc. God wants to give us the opportunity to develop toward the highest state of perfection we are willing to achieve. He wants us to become like Him, to have the same happiness that He enjoys. To do this, He has developed a plan that allows us to come to earth, live in mortal bodies, and have our free will to choose for ourselves the direction we wish to go.

This gift of free will is meaningless unless there is a choice, and in order for there to be a choice, there needed to be two forces, one good and the other evil, pulling in opposite directions. So God created a situation on earth where the opposites, good and evil, exist side by side, forcing us to make millions of decisions, with the goal being to learn to master ourselves and, by choosing good over evil, perfect our character.

Because character development can only occur when a righteous act is performed with no ulterior motive, the plan would require that we be given our free agency, or free choice, to decide for ourselves what we want to do when making decisions involving good or evil. We have also been placed on the earth to be tested, to see if we will exercise enough faith to follow the commandments of God. Those of us who are obedient to the commandments of God and able to perfect our character to a certain point will be the recipients of the gift of eternal life.

Who Would Head the Forces of Good and Evil Here on Earth?

The Old Testament mentioned that there was a spirit in heaven who had achieved high rank and was a great leader of many spirit children of God—that is, until iniquity was found in his heart. It seems this spirit wanted to exalt his throne to be equal to that of God. This caused a war to break out in heaven, and eventually this spirit was cast out from heaven down to earth. The name of this individual was Lucifer, or Satan. On earth he would be given the power to cause such havoc as to shake kingdoms and make the earth tremble. Lucifer's rebellious nature qualified him to play an important part in the plan—a plan where a Messiah would head the forces of good and Lucifer, by choice, would lead the forces of evil.

What Was the Real Significance of What Happened to Adam and Eve in the Garden of Eden?

Since God had given mankind free will, it was essential that the plan be initiated within the framework of free choice. God did not want His spirit children to say we were forced into a world of pain and suffering without any choice on our part. Thus, the plan had to be initiated through an act of free choice, a choice of whether to obey or disobey a commandment with a known penalty. Therefore, the tree of the knowledge of good and evil was placed in the garden of Eden to give Adam and Eve a choice.

They were commanded not to eat from the tree. If they chose to eat the forbidden fruit of the tree, their bodies would become mortal and subject to the opposing forces of good and evil, pleasure and pain, and eventual death.

When Adam and Eve did partake of the forbidden fruit, thus committing a transgression, they not only became aware of good and evil, but became capable of doing evil as well as good. In this state they were separated from the presence of God, because, as the Old Testament tells us, God cannot tolerate evil—or sin.

This enforced separation, then, could be looked upon as a spiritual separation or a type of death. Once Adam and Eve had partaken of the forbidden fruit and had subjected themselves and their future posterity to the effects of sin, the Lord could not allow them to partake again of the fruit of the tree of life. If they had done so, they would have lived forever, with their spirits locked into their mortal bodies in a state of transgression for the rest of eternity. Therefore, they would have lost forever the opportunity to progress and eventually gain a perfect, immortal body and return to the presence of our Father in Heaven.

However, not only did they suffer a spiritual death, or

separation from their Father in Heaven, they would eventually suffer a mortal death, which simply means their bodies would grow old and die. While in this state neither they nor any of their posterity could ever return to their Father in Heaven unless they followed the plan outlined by God.

But Why Couldn't God Just Take Us Back?

God could not just take us back, because once we arrive on earth, all of us, when we reach the age of accountability, will become infected with sin—some to a greater extent than others. If God were to let certain individuals less sinful return to His presence, where would He draw the line? Once a cutoff line is established, the next lower person could always say that he was almost as sin-free as the person just above him. Since one of the attributes of God's character is perfect fairness, the only way for God to resolve the situation was to establish a law that would not allow any of us to return to His presence until we have been cleansed of infectious sin and proved we can obey the laws of the society where God resides.

How Can We Get Back?

God provides commandments as guidelines for us to live by. Whenever we break a divine commandment or law (established to protect freedom, encourage progression, and promote harmony), for justice to be satisfied, we will be required to suffer the penalty, or consequence, attached to that law. The penalty we must suffer will cause a certain amount of pain. Thus, the only way justice can be satisfied is through the inflicting of pain.

However, for justice to be served in this manner poses a problem. It makes no allowance to encourage progression. In fact, it tends to promote regression. For example, as some of us begin committing sins on earth, we can become so weighted down with the pains of those sins that we will want to quit. We will think, "What's the use? If I have to pay for every sin I commit, I might as well quit while I'm ahead."

This is where the Messiah, or Deliverer, comes in. God would select a Messiah and send him to earth for a very special purpose. For those of us who sin and sincerely want to change our ways, there is a way whereby the Messiah can forgive us of our sins, but it has to be done according to the rules of divine law.

Under divine law the Messiah can only forgive after he has paid the price to ransom us from the grasp of justice. The only ransom acceptable is pain. Thus, in order to forgive us of the pain we must suffer, the Messiah must first bear our pain, else he could not forgive us of something he has not paid for. He also has to be without sin. If he sinned, he would no longer be eligible to bear our sins, because he would have to account for his own.

The amount and intensity of pain the Messiah is required to bear, to satisfy the demands of justice, must be great enough so he can forgive, if necessary, millions and millions of people (some of whom will have committed the most heinous crimes).

Once this is accomplished, the responsibility to assure that perfect justice is rendered is transferred from the grasp of justice to the Messiah. In other words, the Messiah now possesses the authority to assess the situation, make allowances for all mitigating/extenuating circumstances, and determine the correct amount of pain each must suffer to resolve the problem.

Whereas, justice is charged with carrying out the letter of the law, the Messiah can now carry out the spirit of the law. Thus, the Messiah can forgive us completely, make us pay the full penalty of pain assigned to that sin, or assign any combination thereof, depending on our change of heart and willingness to follow the commandments of God. The plan must unfold in this manner so that no one could ever accuse the Messiah of forgiving a person, or persons, who may have suffered more pain than the Messiah. Thus, even the smallest requirement of divine law concerning justice and mercy has to be met so God can still say, "I am perfect, and I accomplish all things in accordance with divine laws."

Does the Old Testament Provide Any Clues as to the Identity of the Messiah?

The Old Testament outlined the identity of the Messiah by giving this description of him: The Messiah would come twice, first as a savior, then as a king. The Messiah would be known as the Son of God. His lineage would be from the house of David. During his first sojourn on earth, he would come forth from Bethlehem. He would be born of a virgin. He would grow up as a mortal man. A messenger would prepare the way before him. He would perform incredible miracles.

He would enter Jerusalem riding on a donkey. He would be a man despised and acquainted with grief. He would be betrayed by a friend for thirty pieces of silver. He would be arrested and accused by false witnesses but would not respond to his accusers. He would be smitten and spit upon. He would be affected and brought like a lamb to the slaughter. He would be offered gall and vinegar to drink. Lots would be cast to claim his garments. He would cry out, "My God, my God, why hast thou forsaken me?' He would be put to death for the transgressions of God's people. His bones would not be broken.

He would die with the wicked, but after death his body would rest in a grave with the rich. He would be resurrected and would break the bands of death for all the children of God. And, finally, he would be known as the Redeemer, because he would be wounded for our transgressions.

After he is killed, both Jerusalem and the temple would be destroyed. By his knowledge he would justify many. God will give a portion of His kingdom to him, who would then share it with the righteous. When he would come the second time, it would be as a king. He would establish a kingdom of God on earth and then execute judgment and justice.

Who is the Messiah?

According to the books of the New Testament, the only person in the history of the world to qualify as the Messiah according to the guidelines listed above is Jesus of Nazareth.

What Will Happen to Us After We Die?

One of the most important teachings of the Old Testament is that life continues after our earthly mortal probation is finished, and that the spirits of all mankind can expect to eventually be united with a physical, immortal body composed of flesh and bone. Then a judgment process will take place so that all mankind will be rewarded according to their works and the manner in which they obeyed the commandments of God during their sojourn on earth.

What Will Happen to Individuals Who Will Not Obey the Commandments of God?

Obedience to laws governing mortal life will determine our eligibility and ranking for eternal existence. Mortality is our opportunity to strive to achieve the highest level of eternal existence consistent with our ability to obey divine laws. After life on earth is over, different kingdoms will exist in heaven to house like groups that qualified for like levels of existence. The highest level of existence will be where God resides. To be eligible to return to where God is, we have to prove we can obey the laws of righteousness for that level of existence. Individuals who cannot obey those laws must be segregated so they cannot hinder someone else's progression by infecting or physically/mentally harming them. If we cannot qualify for a higher level, we will be awarded another level commensurate with our ability to obey the laws for that level.

What Is the Judgment Process?

The Messiah will supervise the judgment process so everyone living on earth will receive a just reward and be assigned to the proper level earned by obedience to God's commandments, or laws. To qualify himself for this position, the Messiah had to be exposed to unjust judgment at some point in his life. This is important, so that we can be assured that each of us will receive a fair judgment and will not have to associate with someone who enters into our society unworthily.

This was the basic intricate design of the plan. The plan continually emphasizes the importance of living our lives in a manner worthy to return to the level where God the Father resides. This is called eternal life.

2

Life After Death

What happens after we die? In the Old Testament Isaiah[1] and Hosea[2] wrote that all children of God living on earth will be resurrected. Daniel mentioned that when we are resurrected, some will rise to everlasting life and some to everlasting shame and contempt.[3]

Ecclesiastes mentions that God will bring every work into judgment,[4] and 2 Samuel records that God will reward the doer according to his wickedness.[5]

As to what the righteous could expect, Isaiah said the eye hath not seen what God hath prepared for those that wait upon him.[6] He continues on to explain that God will create a new heaven and a new earth.[7]

From Psalms one learns that it is the righteous who shall inherit this new earth[8] and that the righteous would have a fullness of joy.[9]

---

1. See Isa. 25:8; 26:19
2. See Hos. 13:14
3. See Dan. 12:1
4. See Eccles. 12:14
5 See 2 Sam. 3:39
6. See Isa. 64:4
7. See Isa. 65:17
8. See Psalm 37:9-11
9. See Psalm 16:11

And Daniel said the wise would shine with righteousness.[10]

This is what the Old Testament said about life after death, will the New Testament remain in complete agreement with these concepts while providing more detail concerning each event?

Paradise

To learn what will occur immediately after we die, we need to go to the scriptures and study the events that occurred after Jesus was crucified. This is what is found: When Jesus appeared to Mary Magdalene following his crucifixion and resurrection, he said to Mary, "Touch me not; for I am not yet ascended to my Father: but go to my brethren, and say unto them, I ascend unto my Father, and your Father; and to my God, and your God."[11]

Now, Jesus had been dead for approximately three days before he appeared to Mary Magdalene. If, during this three-day period, he did not return to his Father, where did he go? Jesus answered this question when he said to the thief being crucified next to him, "Verily I say unto thee, *To day shalt thou be with me in paradise.*"[12]

From this, it is evident that when death occurs, the spirits of all mankind enter into the spirit world. Some go to a place called paradise. John says this is a place of rest for the righteous: "Blessed are the dead which die in the Lord from henceforth: yea, saith the Spirit, *that they may rest from their labours; and their works do follow them.*"[13]

But what about individuals who were not righteous, who chose evil instead of good? Speaking about their destination,

---

10. See Daniel 12:3
11. John 20:17
12. Luke 23:43
13. Revelation 14:13

Matthew writes that there is an area called hell and we should not commit acts that could result in our body being cast into hell. [14]

Hell

To explain what hell is like, Peter writes: "Let none of you suffer as a murderer, or as a thief, or as an evildoer, or as a busybody in other men's matters."[15] Isaiah adds: *'The wicked are like the troubled sea, when it cannot rest, whose waters cast up mire and dirt."*[16]

Thus, the minds of the wicked will be continually churned by the thoughts of their unrighteous acts committed during their sojourn here on earth. Jesus tells how intense the pain and suffering is by saying the wicked will be cast into darkness. "There shall be weeping and gnashing of teeth."[17]

Jesus warned the Pharisees, who had derided him, about the exquisite torment one could expect if sent to hell, by telling this parable: "There was a certain rich man, which was clothed in purple and fine linen, and fared sumptuously every day: and there was a certain beggar named Lazarus, which was laid at his gate, full of sores, and desiring to be fed with the crumbs which fell from the rich man's table: moreover the dogs came and licked his sores.

"And it came to pass, that the beggar died, and was carried by the angels into Abraham's bosom: the rich man also died, and was buried; and *in hell he lift up his eyes, being in torments,* and seeth Abraham afar off, and Lazarus in *his* bosom. And he cried and said, Father Abraham, have mercy on me, and send Lazarus, that he may dip the tip of his finger in

---

14. See Matthew 5:29-30
15. 1 Peter 4:15
16. Isaiah 57:20
17. Matthew 8:12

water, and cool my tongue; for I am tormented in this flame.

"But Abraham said, Son, *remember that thou in thy lifetime receivedst thy good things, and likewise Lazarus evil things: but now he is comforted, and thou art tormented.* And beside all this, between us and you there is a great *gulf* fixed: so that they which would pass from hence to you cannot; neither can they pass to us, that would come from thence."[18]

The next five passages tell how the rich man asked Abraham to send Lazarus to warn his five living brothers as to what they can expect if they did not change their ways. But Abraham tells Lazarus his five brothers have their living prophets, and if they will not listen to those prophets, they would not listen to anyone else, even if they rose from the dead.

It is apparent that the richman had allowed his wealth to blind him to the necessity of obeying the commandments of God. Jesus described what hell is like for the wicked. It is a place where the unrighteous endure the cleansing process of pain and suffering to purge their souls of the impurities of unrighteous acts, in order to satisfy the scales of justice.

While reading this story, one cannot help but notice that Jesus mentions a great gulf that existed between the righteous and the wicked in the spirit world: "And beside all this, *between us and you there is a great gulf fixed* so that they which would pass from hence to you cannot; neither can they pass to us, that would come from thence."[19]

From this, it is evident that a barrier has been erected to separate the spirits residing in paradise from the spirits in hell. This passage also tells us that hell is not only a place, but also a state of mind wherein an immortal soul is not only filled with

---

18. Luke 16:19-26.
19. Luke 16:26

anguish, but also is subject to a horrible awareness of ones own guilt. What could cause more mental anguish than knowing that one had the opportunity to achieve the happiness God possesses and lost it by seeking after the vanities of this world?

Spirit Prison

What happens to individuals who are basically good people, but due to events beyond their control had never heard of God the Father or Jesus Christ, nor had any opportunity to learn of their teachings? If God is fair, it seems He would have made some allowance for their condition. Isaiah provides the answer by saying that these particular individuals will be incarcerated in a spirit prison: "They shall be gathered together, as prisoners are gathered in a pit, *and shall be shut up in the prison, and after many days shall they be visited.*"[20]

Who would visit the inhabitants of this spirit prison? Isaiah recorded that the Messiah would accomplish this work: "The spirit of the Lord God is upon me [the Messiah]; because *the Lord hath anointed me to preach good tidings unto the* meek; he hath sent me to bind up the brokenhearted, *to proclaim liberty to the captives, and the opening of the prison to them that are bound.*"[21] Peter confirms Isaiah's comment by saying that Jesus is the one they were waiting for: "Christ also hath once suffered for sins, the just for the unjust, that he might bring us to God, being put to death in the flesh, but quickened by the spirit: by which also *he went and preached unto the spirits in prison.*"[22]

What would Jesus preach when he visited the spirits in prison? Peter said that the spirit prison is a place where the

---
20. Isaiah 24:21-22   22. 1 Peter 3:18-19
21. Isaiah 61:1

Gospel of Jesus Christ is preached to certain individuals who died never having been fully exposed to the commandments of God: *"For this cause was the gospel preached also to them that are dead, that they might be judged according to men in the flesh, but live according to God in the spirit."*[23] This is an important concept, because it means that everyone would eventually have the opportunity to either accept or reject the Gospel.

Since the spirit prison is a place where the Gospel is preached to righteous individuals who died never having been fully exposed to the commandments of God, it means that when they die, the veil blocking remembrance of a premortal life will still exist. This is necessary, because many spirits will still be trying to work out their salvation while residing in the spirit prison.[24]

The Spirit World

From this information it is apparent that, following mortal death, spirits are consigned to separate locations in the spirit world, depending on their state of righteousness or wickedness.

Jesus foretold his visit to the spirit world and spirit prison by telling the scribes and Phasees who asked for a sign: "There shall be no sign given...but the sign of the prophet Jonas: *for as Jonas was three days and three nights in the whale's belly; so shall the Son of man be three days and three nights in the heart of the earth."*[25] Thus, while his dead body was in the grave, Jesus himself spent three days ministering in the spirit world before he appeared to Mary Magdalene as a resurrected being.[26]

---

23. 1 Peter 4:6
24. See Philippians 2:12
25. Matthew 12:40
26. See John 20:17

The Spirit World Is a Temporary Holding Area

The prophet Hosea knew that the spirit world is only a temporary holding area. He said the Messiah would eventually release all individuals from its confines: *"'I [the Messiah] will ransom them from the power of the grave; I will redeem them from death: O death, I will be thy plagues; O grave, I will be thy destruction."*[27]

Jesus said he will be the one to unlock the gates of hell and death: *"I am he that liveth, and was dead; and behold, I am alive for evermore, Amen; and have the keys of hell and of death."*[28]

In his vision of the resurrection, John writes: *"The sea gave up the dead which were in it; and death and hell delivered up the dead which were in them: and they were judged every man according to their works."*[29]

Resurrection

What does it mean to be resurrected? This is the process whereby the body is reunited with the spirit. The prophet Ezekiel gives a graphic description of the resurrection process. Though his vision is considered to refer only to the dead house of Israel, it is a true representation, for the Lord says: *"When I have opened your graves, O my people, and brought you up out of your graves, and shall put my spirit in you.. Ye shall live."*[30] And the apostle Paul explains that when a person is resurrected, the spirit will be united with an immortal body: *"This mortal shall have put on immortality, then shall be brought to pass the saying that is written, Death is swallowed up in victory."*[31]

---

27. Hosea 13:14
28. Revelation 1:18
29. Revelation 20:13
30. See Ezekiel 37:13-14
31. 1 Corinthians 15:54

What is an immortal body like? To find the answer, it is necessary to study John's comments concerning what happened when Jesus appeared to his disciples following his resurrection: "As they thus spake, Jesus himself stood in the midst of them, and saith unto them, Peace be unto you. But they were terrified and affrighted, and supposed that they had seen a spirit. And he said unto them, Why are ye troubled? and why do thoughts arise in your hearts? *Behold my hands and my feet, that it is I myself: handle me, and see: for a spirit hath not flesh and bones, as ye see me have.*"[32] From this, it is evident that Jesus appeared before his disciples in a body of flesh and bones and spirit. By all appearances this body looked normal. Jesus even challenged his disciples to feel it. He then demonstrated the reality of his body by eating a piece of broiled fish and honeycomb.

Though his resurrected body appeared the same as before his death, it was not, because Jesus had suddenly materialized in front of his disciples out of thin air. This tells us that an immortal body looks and feels much the same as a mortal body but has the ability to move through the air, pass through walls, and appear or disappear on command of its owner.

Thus, an immortal body is not subject to the normal physical laws governing earthly matter as we know it. Another feature of an immortal body is that it will not grow old and die, but will last forever.

Though the body that Jesus displayed to his disciples was his immortal body, it was not in its glorified state. The book of Revelation tells us what the glorified body of Jesus Christ looks like: "In the midst of the seven candlesticks one like unto the

---

32. Luke 24:36-39

Son of man, clothed with a garment down to the foot, and girt about the paps with a golden girdle. *His head and his hairs were white like wool, as white as snow; and his eyes were as a flame of fire; and his feet like unto fine brass, as if they burned in a furnace, and his voice as the sound of many waters...* And when I saw him, I fell at his feet as dead. And he laid his right hand upon me saying unto me, Fear not; I am the first and the last: I am he that liveth, and was dead; and, behold, *I am alive for evermore, Amen; and have the keys of hell and of death."*[33]

This is an important precept, because it tells us what kind of body God the Father possesses. For example, Jesus said, *"He that hath seen* me *hath seen the Father."*[34] As mentioned previously, Jesus could make this comment, just as Seth, the son of Adam, was qualified to say, If ye see me, ye have seen my father, Adam—because the scriptures tell us that Adam *"begat a son in his own likeness, after his image; and called his name Seth."*[35]

Thus, when Jesus said, When you have seen me, you have seen my Father, he is saying, in essence, my Father has a body exactly like mine.

Will Jesus Christ ever again be separated from his immortal body? The scriptures define physical death as the separation of the body from the spirit. Paul said, Now that Jesus Christ is resurrected with an immortal body, he will never taste of death. In other words, his body will never again be separated from his spirit: "Knowing *that Christ being raised from the dead dieth no more; death hath no more dominion over him. For in that he died, he died unto sin once: but in that he liveth, he liveth unto God."*[36]

---

33. Revelation 1:13-18, 2:18
34. John 14:9
35. Genesis 5:3
36. Romans 6:9

Knowing that the spirit of Jesus Christ could never again be separated from his immortal body gives us another important insight concerning his earthly mission. Since God the Father has a body exactly like that of His Son, Jesus Christ, His spirit also could never be separated from His immortal body. The important concept to be gleaned is this: the scriptures tell us that only two individuals were qualified (by perfection) to perform the mission of being a savior to the human race. These two individuals were God the Father and His Son, Jesus Christ.

Why did our Father in Heaven delegate this job to His Son? The above information gives us the key. God could not come to earth and give His life, because He already had an immortal body. And the scriptures tell us that once the immortal body is united with the spirit, it can never again be separated. Thus, since Jesus Christ had not yet received his immortal body, he was the only one who could fulfill this mission.

Who Will Be Resurrected?

Isaiah mentioned that all of God's children would be resurrected.[37] Does the New Testament agree with this statement? Paul confirms it by saying: "Since by man came death, by man came also the resurrection of the dead. For as in Adam *all die,* even so in Christ shall *all be made alive.*"[38]

When Adam transgressed the commandment of God by partaking of the fruit of the tree of knowledge of good and evil, he brought death into the world. When Jesus Christ sacrificed his life upon the cross, he made it possible for all mankind to be resurrected with an immortal body. Some Bible scholars have expressed the belief that only the righteous are resur-

---

37. See Isaiah 26:19
38. 1 Corinthians 15:21-22

rected with an immortal body; however, Daniel mentioned that when we are resurrected, some will rise to everlasting life and some to everlasting shame and contempt.[39] Does the New Testament agree with this?

This statement is recorded by John: "Marvel not at this: for the hour is coming, in the which *all that are in the graves* shall hear his [Jesus'] voice, and shall come forth; they that have done good, unto the resurrection of life; and they that have done evil, unto the resurrection of damnation."[40]

So far, the Old Testament and New Testament seem to correspond exactly.

Can we expect to have the same kind of immortal body of flesh and bone that Christ displayed to his disciples? Job answers this question in the affirmative by saying that though his mortal body would die and rot away, some day his spirit would once again be clothed with an immortal body of flesh and bone, thus enabling him to gaze upon God: *"Though after my skin worms destroy this body, yet in my flesh shall I see God.* "[41]

But can the righteous expect to receive a body exactly like the glorified body Jesus Christ exhibited? The first indication that this will happen comes from the prophet Daniel as he says, "They that be wise *shall shine as the brightness of the firmament; and they that turn many to righteousness as the stars for ever and ever."*[42] Thus, those who are wise by doing the will of God and those who use their talents to build the kingdom of God on earth by turning many towards righteousness will shine as the stars forever and ever.

Paul confirms Daniel's statement by saying, unequivocally, that the righteous can expect to have a body fashioned

---

39. See Daniel 12:2
40. John 5:28-29
41. Job 19:26
42. Daniel 12:3

after Jesus' glorious body: "Our conversation is in heaven; from whence also we look for the Saviour, the Lord Jesus Christ: *who shall change our vile body, that it may be fashioned like unto his glorious body,* according to the working whereby he is able even to subdue all things to himself."[43] John also supports Daniel's and Paul's comments by saying: "Beloved, now are we the sons of God, and it doth not yet appear what we shall be: *but we know that, when he shall appear, we shall be like him; for we shall see him as he is."*[44]

Will we ever again suffer a physical death by having our spirits separated from our immortal body? Christ explains that once our physical body is reunited with our spirit during the resurrection process, it can never be separated: *"Neither can they [all mankind] die any more: for they are equal unto the angels; and are the children of God, being the children of the resurrection."*[45]

In What Order Will the Resurrection Occur?

Paul recorded that there would be an order by which all individuals will be resurrected: *"Every man in his own order: Christ the firstfruits; afterward they that are Christ's at his coming.* Then cometh the end, when he shall have delivered up the kingdom to God, even the Father."[46] Christ was the first to be resurrected. The next group to be resurrected would be they *"that are Christ's at his coming,"*[47] meaning at the second coming of Jesus Christ.

But what about the small resurrection that occurred just after Christ was resurrected two thousand years ago: *"The graves were opened; and many bodies of the saints which slept*

---

43. Philippians 3:20-21
44. 1 John 3:2
45. Luke 20:36
46. 1 Cor. 15:23-24
47. 1 Cor. 15:23

LIFE AFTER DEATH

arose, and came out of the graves after his resurrection, and went into the holy city, and appeared unto many."[48]

Apparently this mini-resurrection was a preview of what to expect and to show that the bands of death had been broken, not only for Jesus Christ, but for all of God's children. It is not to be confused with the first general resurrection, to occur just prior to the Second Coming.

Participants of the First Resurrection

Who will participate in the first general resurrection? Paul told the Thessalonians these would be they who died in Christ: *"The Lord himself shall descend from heaven with a shout, with the voice of the archangel, and with the trump of God: and the dead in Christ shall rise first."*[49] What did Paul mean by saying "the dead in Christ"? The answer, according to Jesus, is *"they that have done good"*[50] in obeying the commandments of God. This corresponds with the comment of King David in the Old Testament that God will "reward the doer according to his wickedness."[51] John the Revelator adds this thought: "Blessed and holy is he that hath part in the first resurrection: *on such the second death hath* no *power,* but they shall be priests of God and of Christ, and shall reign with him a thousand years."[52] Note: in this case the second death refers to the separation of the individual from God the Father.

Thus, those righteous individuals who kept the commandments of God will be resurrected at the second coming of Christ and will reign with him for one thousand years. But what about the wicked? When will they be resurrected?

---

48. Mat. 27:52-53
49. 1 Thes. 4:16
50. John 5:29
51. See 2 Sam. 3:39
52. Rev. 20:6

Resurrection of the Wicked

To answer this question, we need to turn to the book of Revelation. Here we learn that the wicked will have to wait at least one thousand years. Listen to the words of John: "I saw the souls of them that were beheaded for the witness of Jesus, and for the word of God...and they lived and reigned with Christ a thousand years. *But the rest of the dead lived not again until the thousand years were finished.*"[53]

What will be the status of Satan during this thousand-year period. From the book of Revelation we read that Satan will be bound and cast in a pit, unable to deceive the nations of the earth until the thousand-year period was over.

John said, *"I saw an angel come down from heaven, having the key of the bottomless pit and a great chain in his hand. And he laid hold on the dragon, that old serpent, which is the Devil and Satan, and bound him a thousand years, and cast him into the bottomless pit, and shut him up, and set a seal upon him, that he should deceive the nations no more, till the thousand years should be fulfilled."*[54]

The thousand-year period when Satan will be cast into prison is called the Millennium. This is the time when, Micah says, that peace and prosperity will reign over the earth: "They shall beat their swords into plowshares, and their spears into pruninghooks; nation shall not lift up a sword against nation, neither shall they learn war any more."[55]

After the Thousand-Year Period of Peace and Prosperity

What happens after the thousand-year period of peace and

---

53. Revelation 20:4-5
54. Revelation 20:1-3
55. Micah 4:3

prosperity is completed? Revelation states that when the Millennium is over, Satan will be released from prison to again wreak havoc and vengeance upon the earth. One last great battle will occur between the saints of God and the hosts of Satan. Then Satan and his followers will be subdued by the power of God.

John reports: *"When the thousand years are expired, Satan shall be loosed out of his prison, and shall go out to deceive the nations which are in the four quarters of the earth, Gog and Magog, to gather them together in battle: the number of whom is as the sand of the sea. And they went up on the breadth of the earth, and compassed the camp of the saints about, and the beloved city: and fire came down from God out of heaven, and devoured them."*[56]

After Satan and his hosts have been permanently subdued, the stage is set for the final judgment.

Final Judgment

Graduations are always exciting, whether it be from high school, college, the university, or some other hard fought endeavor. For the student, it is a time of relief, nostalgia, appreciation, sense of accomplishment, understanding, happiness and joy.

It is a time of closeness with fellow students who have shared the good times and bad. It is a time when brothers, sisters, relatives, and friends gather around to help celebrate the victory. It is a time when proud parents sit in commencement exercises and wipe away tears of happiness as their children walk forward to accept hard-earned diplomas.

---

56. Revelation 20:7-9

It is a time when concerned teachers feel a sense of accomplishment as they contemplate their part in the growth that has taken place in individual students.

It is a time when special awards are given out to those students who distinguished themselves in various mental and physical pursuits. It is a time of speeches, advice for the attainment of future goals, congratulations, peace, love, and joy.

But graduations can also be a time of sadness, sorrow, pain and suffering for those individuals who enrolled in the classes but failed to finish the curriculum. Unfortunately, this pain and sorrow affects, not only the individual student, but all those who have expended the time and effort to help, such as friends, relatives, teachers, and parents. Feelings of failure, disgrace, loss of opportunity and self-respect will haunt the soul after the sounds of the graduation ceremonies have been stilled, and this haunting will continue to echo its message of failure down the hallways of the mind for years to come.

Yes, graduations are a very special time, but the greatest graduation of all is yet to take place. This graduation is called "The great final judgment" For those individuals who endure to the end, it will be the greatest and most joyous event to ever occur within their lives. In many ways this gathering will be very similar to a graduation ceremony held on earth.

This is the event, spoken about in both the Old and New Testaments, that will occur after the end of the Millennium, or the thousand-year period of peace and prosperity, and after Satan and his followers have finally been subdued by the power of God. This is the event that will ring down the curtain on the final stage of our earthly mortal life.

At this final judgment will be gathered together every soul that has ever lived on the face of the earth, to stand before God and receive his or her just reward.

By this time, all mankind will have been resurrected with an immortal body. This immortal body is a gift to each of us as a result of the atoning sacrifice of Jesus Christ. Some individuals will have been resurrected with an immortal body over a thousand years before. These are the righteous who were with Christ at his second coming. Others will have just received this gift after having been released from a thousand years in hell.

Some of the participants will be dressed in exquisite white robes and gowns. The white clothing will identify those who have taken advantage of the process of repentance and were cleansed from all iniquity by the blood of the Lamb.

Within this vast body of souls will stand the valiant: Adam, Enoch, Noah, Abraham, Moses, and the rest of the prophets, along with all of the faithful followers of Jesus Christ. But here also will be seen the infamous: Cain, Judas, Nero, Hitler, Stalin, and all those who joined forces with the adversary to overthrow and destroy the works of God.

This judgment will occur under the direction of Jesus Christ: *"The Father judgeth no man, but hath committed all judgment unto the Son."*[57] Paul confirms this by saying, *"We must all appear before the judgment seat of Christ; that every one may receive the things done in his body, according to that he hath done, whether it be good or bad."*[58] Paul also mentions that the standard by which all men will be judged is the Gospel of Jesus Christ: "...in the day when *God shall judge the secrets of men by Jesus Christ according to my gospel."*[59]

---

57. John 5:22
58. 2 Corinthians 5:10
59. Romans 2:16

What happens next is described by John: "I saw the dead, small and great, stand before God; and the books were opened: and another book was opened, which is the book of life: *and the dead were judged out of those things which were written in the books, according to their works.* And the sea gave up the dead which were in it; and death and hell delivered up the dead which were in them: *and they were judged every man according to their works.*"[60]

Matthew adds the words of Jesus: *"Before him [the Son of man] shall be gathered all nations: and he shall separate them one from another,* as a shepherd divideth his sheep from the goats: and he shall set the sheep on his right hand, but the goats on the left."[61]

The book of life will contain a complete record of all our righteous accomplishments and our deficiencies. Our works mentioned in this book will determine our destiny for the rest of eternity. When this occurs, the time will be too late for individuals to change. The decisions we made while living on earth and in the spirit world will have been indelibly engraven into the Lamb's book of life. This will be the time when we will review our lives, and those of us who spent our lives in pursuit of doing the will of God will be able to see that God knew every flaw within our souls, what capabilities we possessed, and how to enhance our capabilities by the blows of the hammer of tribulation. We will stand as a living testimony, a finished masterpiece modeled by the hands of the master sculptor.

Reading further in Matthew, we can gain more of an understanding of exactly what Jesus means by the term "works" mentioned in the book of life:

---

60. Revelation 20:12-13
61. Matthew 25:32-33

"Before him [the Son of man] shall be gathered all nations: and he shall separate them one from another, as a shepherd divideth his sheep from the goats: and he shall set the sheep on his right hand, but the goats on the left.

"Then shall the King say unto them on his right hand, Come, ye blessed of my Father, inherit the kingdom prepared for you from the foundation of the world: *For I was an hungred, and ye gave me meat: I was thirsty, and ye gave me drink: I was a stranger, and ye took me in: naked, and ye clothed me: I was sick, and ye visited me: I was in prison, and ye came unto me.*

"Then shall the righteous answer him, saying, Lord, when saw we thee an hungred, and fed thee? or thirsty, and gave thee drink? When saw we thee a stranger, and took thee in? or naked, and clothed thee? Or when saw we thee sick, or in prison, and came unto thee? And the King shall answer and say unto them, *Verily I say unto you, Inasmuch as ye have done it unto one of the least of these my brethren, ye have done it unto me.*"[62]

In addition to the above, Jesus gave us three parables which better explain who will inherit the kingdom of heaven.

Parable of the Ten Virgins

"Then shall the kingdom of heaven be likened unto ten virgins, which took their lamps, and went forth to meet the bridegroom. And five of them were wise, and five were foolish. They that were foolish took their lamps, and took no oil with them: but the wise took oil in their vessels with their lamps. While the bridegroom tarried, they all slumbered and slept. And at midnight there was a cry made, Behold, the bridegroom cometh; go ye out to meet him.

---
62. Matthew 25:32-40

"Then all those virgins arose, and trimmed their lamps. And the foolish said unto the wise, Give us of your oil; for our lamps are gone out. But the wise answered, saying, Not so; lest there be not enough for us and you: but go ye rather to them that sell, and buy for yourselves. And while they went to buy, the bridegroom came; and they that were ready went in with him to the marriage: and the door was shut. Afterward came also the other virgins, saying, Lord, Lord, open to us. But he answered and said, Verily I say unto you, I know you not."[63]

From this scripture it is apparent that the ten virgins represent believers in Jesus Christ, and the oil represents the diligence with which they obeyed the commandments of God.

The five virgins who were wise represent believers in Jesus Christ who have filled their lamps with the oil of faith and good works by obeying the commandments of God and promoting the kingdom of God on earth. Thus, it was the light of righteousness that enabled them to go out into the dark and find their bridegroom.

The five virgins who were foolish represent believers in Jesus Christ who have not kept their lamps filled with the oil of faith and good works, but instead sit complacently idle, thinking all is well. These are they whom Jesus classified as being lukewarm in living and furthering the work of God on earth.[64] For he said, *"Not every one that saith unto me, Lord, Lord, shall enter into the kingdom of heaven; but he that doeth the will of my Father which is in heaven."*[65]

Parable of the Talents

"The kingdom of heaven is as a man traveling into a far

---

63. Matthew 25:1-12
64. Revelation 3:15
65. Matthew 7:21

country, who called his own servants, and delivered unto them his goods. And unto one he gave five talents, to another two, and to another one; to every man according to his several ability; and straightway took his journey. Then he that had received the five talents went and traded with the same, and made them other five talents. And likewise he that had received two, he also gained other two. But he that had received one went and digged in the earth, and hid his lord's money.

"After a long time the lord of those servants cometh, and reckoneth with them. And so he that had received five talents came and brought other five talents, saying, Lord, thou deliveredst unto me five talents: behold, I have gained beside them five talents more. His lord said unto him, Well done, thou good and faithful servant: thou hast been faithful over a few things, I will make thee ruler over many things: enter thou into the joy of thy lord.

"He also that had received two talents came and said, Lord, thou deliveredst unto me two talents: behold, I have gained two other talents beside them. His Lord said unto him, Well done, good and faithful servant; thou hast been faithful over a few things, I will make thee ruler over many things: enter thou into the joy of thy lord.

"When he which had received the one talent came and said, Lord, I knew thee that thou art an hard man, reaping where thou hast not sown, and gathering where thou hast not strawed: and I was afraid, and went and hid my talent in the earth: lo, there thou hast that is thine.

"His lord answered and said unto him, Thou wicked and slothful servant, thou knewest that I reap where I sowed not, and gather where I have not strawed: thou oughtest therefore to have put my money to the exchangers, and then at my coming I should have received mine own with usury. Take therefore the talent from him, and give it unto him which hath ten talents. For unto every one that hath shall be given, and he shall have abundance: but from him that hath not shall be taken away even that which he hath. And cast ye the unprofitable servant into outer darkness; there shall be weeping and gnashing of teeth."[66]

This parable says we should develop the talents God has blessed us with. What better way is there to explain that our purpose for coming to earth is to develop our internal qualities to become a more perfect person, than by this parable? When this thought is combined with the first parable, it tells us we can develop these qualities by following the commandments of God.

Here on earth many people will sacrifice their personal integrity in order to rise to positions of authority. In the life beyond the veil, once Jesus comes into his power, those who will rule with him will be they who maintained their personal integrity while undergoing the tribulations of earth life. The governing body in the celestial realms of heaven will be almost a total reversal of what has occurred on earth.

Parable of the Marriage Feast

To erase all doubt concerning who will be allowed into the kingdom of heaven, Matthew recorded a third parable: the parable of the marriage feast.

"The kingdom of heaven is like unto a certain king, which made a marriage for his son, and sent forth his servants to call

---

66. Matthew 25:14-30

them that were bidden to the wedding: and they would not come. Again, he sent forth other servants, saying, Tell them which are bidden, Behold, I have prepared my dinner: my oxen and my fatlings are killed, and all things are ready: come unto the marriage.

"But they made light of it, and went their ways, one to his farm, another to his merchandise: and the remnant took his servants, and entreated them spitefully, and slew them. But when the king heard thereof, he was wroth: and he sent forth his armies, and destroyed those murderers, and burned up their city.

"Then saith he to his servants, The wedding is ready, but they which were bidden were not worthy. Go ye therefore into the highways, and as many as ye shall find, bid to the marriage. So those servants went out into the highways, and gathered together all as many as they found, both bad and good: and the wedding was furnished with guests.

"And when the king came in to see the guests, he saw there a man which had not a wedding garment: and he saith unto him, Friend how camest thou in hither not having a wedding garment? And he was speechless. Then said the king to the servants, Bind him hand and foot, and take him away, and cast him into outer darkness; there shall be weeping and gnashing of teeth. For many are called, but few are chosen."[67]

The marriage feast is a time when the bridegroom can meet and rejoice with both his expectant bride and the friends who will assist him when he inherits his kingdom. Jesus said that the invitation sent from the king represents the Gospel, that the Gospel would be taken first to the house of Israel, to

---

67. Matthew 22:2-14

accept or reject, and then to the Gentiles.

"These twelve [apostles] Jesus sent forth, and commanded them, saying, *Go not into the way of the Gentiles, and into any city of the Samaritans enter ye not: but go rather to the lost sheep of the house of Israel.*"[68] Later Jesus said why he did this *"I am not sent but unto the lost sheep of the house of Israel."*[69] Also: "Think not that I am come to destroy the law, or the prophets: I am not come to destroy, but to fulfill."[70]

After the gospel had been given first to the house of Israel, it was then given to the Gentiles, as confirmed by these words of Peter to Cornelius: *"Ye know how that it is an unlawful thing for a man that is a Jew to keep company, or come unto one of another nation; but God hath shewed me that I should not call any man common or unclean....While Peter yet spake these words, the Holy Ghost fell on all them which heard the word. And they of the circumcision which believed were astonished, as many as came with Peter, because that on the Gentiles also was poured our the gift of the Holy Ghost. For they heard them speak with tongues, and magnify God. Then answered Peter, Can any man forbid water, that these should not be baptized, which have received the Holy Ghost as well as we? And he commanded them to be baptized in the name of the Lord.* Then prayed they him to tarry certain days."[71]

This information helps us to understand why Jesus said, *"Many that are first shall be last; and the last first."*[72] Paul put it more succinctly: "Glory, honour, and peace, to every man that worketh good, *to the Jew first, and also to the Gentile: for there is no respect of persons with God.*"[73]

Also in his parable of the marriage feast an interesting

---

68. Matthew 10:5-6
69. Matthew 15:24
70. Matthew 5:17
71. Acts 10:28-48
72. Mark 10:31
73. Romans 2:10-11

comment was made by the king when he observed the clothing worn by one of the guests; "he saw there a man which had not on a wedding garment: and he saith unto him *Friend, how camest thou hither not having a wedding garment? And he was speechless. Then said the king to the servants, Bind him hand and foot, and take him away, and cast him into outer darkness; there shall be weeping and gnashing of teeth.*"[74]

What is the significance of the wedding agreement? The answer is found in revelation: "One of the elders answered, saying unto me, *What are these which are arrayed in white robes? and whence came they?* And I said unto him, Sir, thou knowest. And he said to me, *These are they which came out of great tribulation, and have washed their robes, and made them white in the blood of the Lamb.*"[75] Then, again in Revelation, John adds: "Let us be glad and rejoice, and give honour to him: for the marriage of the Lamb is come, and his wife hath made herself ready. And to her was granted that she should be arrayed in fine linen, clean and white: for the fine linen is the righteousness of saints...blessed are they which are called unto the marriage supper of the Lamb."[76]

In this passage we have the answers to three important questions.

First, the white linen represents the righteousness of the individuals who have completed the tribulations of earth life and have taken advantage of the blood atonement of Jesus Christ by complying with the principles of the Gospel.

Second, the bride represents Christ's Church.

Third, an individual in the parable of the marriage feast was not wearing the garment of righteousness; therefore, he

---

74. Matthew 22:11-13
75. Revelation 7:13-14
76. Revelation 19:7-9

was not allowed to remain with the wedding party. Concerning this, Jesus said, *"The Son of man shall send forth his angels, and they shall gather out of his kingdom all things that offend, and them which do iniquity;* and shall cast them into a furnace of fire: there shall be wailing and gnashing of teeth. Then shall the righteous shine forth as the sun in the kingdom of their Father."[77]

In this parable of the marriage feast, the prince, or son of the king, also deserves some comment. Here the prince (the Messiah, Jesus Christ) represents the rightful future heir to the kingdom of His Father. In other words, he is the future king and thus will possess all the power, wealth, and glory associated with the rank of king. As mentioned previously, the guests represents the faithful saints of Christ's Church and, as such, will rule and reign over the kingdom alongside Christ.

However, while the prince obtained his position by rightful lineage garnered through perfect obedience, it will be necessary for the saints to qualify through the combined elements of righteous works and by the acceptance or grace of the prince before they can be appointed to positions of authority. An interesting point to glean from this parable is that a common righteous person has the opportunity to rise from nothing to a position of great power, dominion, wealth, and glory.

Though this parable was spoken two thousand years ago, this dream is harbored in the hearts of many Americans, as demonstrated by our insatiable desire to know all the intimate details of the engagements, weddings, and happenings within the royal family of Great Britain.

We even try to put some of our own American citizens on

---

77. Matthew 13:41-48

the pedestal of royalty. In the 1960s the idea of Camelot within our political structure appealed to many. Many of the stars of Hollywood are considered by their fans to be royalty.

In fact, the American dream has been demonstrated time and again by thousands of our ancestors who have immigrated to the United States with very little money and have risen to positions of power. But the irony of this concept is that, while many fantasize and harbor these intense feelings within their hearts, very few think they stand much chance of ever attaining such a prized position.

Yet this is really what the plan of our Father in Heaven is all about. The plan is designed so every person living on earth has the opportunity to become co-heirs with Jesus Christ and join with him as he rules in the kingdom of heaven. All it takes is steadfastness in obeying his commandments. These are the works the righteous will perform.

These are they who have proven they can obey the commandments of God from behind the veil of faith. These are they who have cleansed their garments in the blood of the Lamb by taking advantage of the principle of repentance.

These are they who understand that freedom must be protected by laws so it can function properly and that the amount of freedom a person is able to enjoy is contingent upon the laws he is willing to obey. These are they who understand the constraints placed by laws on someone who is perfect and governs by laws. These are they who understand that survival of good government is directly related to the ethics, integrity, morality, and righteousness of its citizens.

These are they who have learned that the only way to lead is by setting the perfect example in all things. These are they who have finally learned that righteousness encourages progression, whereas evil inhibits progression. These are they who want to dedicate their lives toward organizing the elements of matter into things of beauty that uplift the soul.

These are they who have learned that progression only occurs when it is carried out under the plan of our Father in Heaven. These are they who have finally learned that when our future is left in the hands of mortal man, all will eventually end in destruction. These are they who, after experiencing the forging heat of earth life, have demonstrated they can live in God's kingdom and still not infect with sin His other innocent children who have not yet experienced the classroom of earth life.

These are they who have developed their character traits in accordance with the gospel principles of love and service to others, thus demonstrating that they have developed the integrity to be trusted with perfect knowledge, power, and authority so they can govern in the far corners of God's kingdom.

These are they who have proven they can perpetuate the kingdom of God by righteously promulgating eternal life.

These are they who, while standing before the judgment bar of God, will experience the sweet satisfaction of hearing their Savior say, *"Come, ye blessed of my Father, inherit the kingdom prepared for you from the foundation of the world."*[78]

But what about the wicked and the unrighteous? What can they expect to happen during the final judgment? These individuals will review their past lives that day and will experience feelings of futility, absurdness, and despair. For at that moment their decision to follow after worldly pleasures will impact completely upon their consciousness.

---
78. Matthew 25:34

What are the 'works" of the unrighteous? Matthew recorded Jesus' answer: "Then shall he say also unto them on the left hand, Depart from me ye cursed, into everlasting fire, prepared for the devil and his angels: *For I was an hungred, and* ye *gave* me no meat *I was thirsty, and ye gave* me no *drink: I was* a stranger, and ye took me not in: naked, *and* ye *clothed* me not: *sick,* and in prison, and ye *visited* me *not.*

"'Then shall they also answer him, saying, Lord, when saw we thee an hungred, or athirst, or a stranger, or naked, or sick, or in prison, and did not minister unto thee?

"Then shall he answer them, saying, Verily I say unto you, Inasmuch as ye did it not to one of the least of these, ye did it not to me. And these shall go away into everlasting punishment: but the righteous into life eternal."[79]

From Jesus' Sermon on the Mount recorded by Matthew, we learn more as to how people will respond to the final judgment: *"Many will say to me in that day, Lord,* Lord, *have we not prophesied in thy name? and in thy name have* cast *out devils? and in thy name* done *many wonderful works? And then will I profess unto them, I never knew you: depart from me, ye that work iniquity."*[80]

These are they who spurned the commandments and prophets of God in order to gratify their own appetites of flesh and greed. These are they who lived their lives in search of praise, acquiring money or seducing women and experiencing whatever the world had to offer.

These are they who could not accept the existence of God the Father or His Son Jesus Christ on faith only. These are they who must now be segregated into a reduced level of freedom, corresponding to the laws they were willing to obey on earth.

---

79. Matthew 25:41-46
80. Matthew 7:22-23

These are they who did not overcome the effects of living within the forces of good and evil and, therefore, cannot be trusted to live in the area of God's kingdom where they can infect His other innocent children with sin.

These are they who were never able to develop the integrity of character to handle perfect knowledge, power, and authority. Their inheritance will be limited to the level of integrity developed.

These are they who are not eligible to perpetuate the kingdom of God and promulgate eternal life. These are they who had their chance and failed and now must live with this knowledge for the rest of eternity.

These are they who, while standing before the judgment bar of God, will hear these stinging words: *"Depart from me, ye cursed, into everlasting fire, prepared for the devil and his angels"*[81]

After the Final Judgment

Where do we go after the final judgment? While some Bible scholars have depicted life after the last judgment as consisting solely of a heaven and hell, Jesus painted a different picture, for he said to his disciples: *"In my Father's house are many mansions:* if it were not so, I would have told you. I go to prepare a place for you. And if I go and prepare a place for you, I will come again, and receive you unto myself; that where I am, there ye may be also."[82] In this passage Jesus is saying that there are many places to which individuals may be assigned after the final judgment.

Paul sheds more light on this subject by explaining that

---

81. Matthew 25-41
82. John 14:2-3

the kingdom of God is divided into three primary sub-kingdoms. The first kingdom is compared to the splendor of the sun; the second, to the moon; and the third, to the stars. He further explains that all mankind, once resurrected, will be divided into three groups. The first group is compared in splendor to the sun; the second to the moon; and the third to the differing glories of the stars, thus indicating that each group will inherit a like kingdom.

From this, we can expect to see the most righteous group assigned to the kingdom with the glory of the sun; the second most righteous group to the kingdom with the glory of the moon; and the third to the kingdom with the glory of the stars. This is how Paul describes it: "There is *one glory of the sun, and another glory of the moon, and another glory of the stars: for one star differeth from another star in glory. So also is the resurrection of the dead.*"[83]

Paul names two of these three kingdoms: "There are also *celestial bodies,* and *bodies terrestrial:* but *the glory of the celestial* is *one, and the glory of the terrestrial* is *another.*"[84] Thus, one kingdom is called celestial and the second is called terrestrial.

Celestial Kingdom

Who will inherit the celestial kingdom? John recorded this: *"Blessed are they that* do *his commandments,* that they may have the right to the tree of life, and may enter in through the gates into the city."[85]

And what is their reward? Isaiah said the eye hath not

---

83. 1 Corinthians 15:41-42
84. 1 Corinthians 15:40
85. Revelation 22:14

seen what God hath prepared for those that wait upon him[86] and that God will create a new heaven and a new earth for His people.[87]

Does the New Testament corroborate Isaiah's statement? John the Revelator said, *"I saw a new heaven and a new earth:* for the first heaven and the first earth were passed away; and there was no more sea.

"And I John saw the holy city, new Jerusalem, coming down from God out of heaven, prepared as a bride adorned for her husband. And I heard a great voice out of heaven saying, Behold, the tabernacle of God is with men, and he will dwell with them, and they shall be his people, and God himself shall be with them, and be their God.

"And God *shall* wipe *away all tears from their eyes; and there shall be no more death, neither sorrow, nor crying, neither shall there be any more pain:* for the former things are passed away.

"And he that sat upon the throne said, Behold *I make all things* new. And he said unto me, Write: for these words are true and faithful.. And he said unto me, It is done. I am Alpha and Omega, the beginning and the end. *I will give unto him that* is *athirst of the fountain of the water of life freely. He that overcometh shall inherit all things:* and I will be his God, and he shall be my son"[88]

To this, the Savior adds: *"To him that overcometh will I grant to sit with me in my throne, even as I also overcame, and am set down with my Father in his throne."*[89] And, finally, the words of the Psalmist tell what it will be like to be in the presence of Jesus Christ and God the Father: *"In thy presence* is *fullness of joy; at thy right hand there are plea-*

---

86. See Isaiah 64:4
87. See Isaiah 65:17
88. Revelation 21:1-7
89. Revelation 3:21

sures for evermore."[90]

And what gift will the righteous receive in this kingdom? The apostle Paul, *in* a letter *to* Timothy, says it is eternal life: "Fight the good fight of faith, lay hold on eternal life,"[91] and confirms this in his letter to the Romans: "The wages of sin is death; but the gift of God is eternal life through Jesus Christ our Lord."[92]

The Terrestrial Kingdom

Who will inherit the terrestrial kingdom? As Paul stated, these are they whose reward or glory will differ from those who inherit the celestial kingdom as the glory of the sun differs from the moon. These are they who, like the five unprepared virgins, are good people but were not valiant in the testimony of Jesus Christ and, as a result, may be the people Jeremiah was referring to when he said, *"The harvest is past, the summer is ended, and we are not saved."*[93]

The Third Kingdom

Who will inherit the third kingdom? John said, "Without *are dogs, and sorcerers, and whoremongers, and murderers, and idolaters, and whosoever loveth and maketh a lie."*[94]

Thus, the unrighteous must serve at least one thousand years in the spirit prison, undergoing the cleansing process of pain and suffering to purge their souls of the impurities of unrighteous acts, to satisfy the scales of justice.

Jesus put it this way: *"Verily I say unto thee, Thou shalt by no means come out thence [from prison], till thou hast paid the uttermost farthing."*[95] Once released from prison, they will

---

90. Psalm 16:11
91. 1 Timothy 6:12
92: Romans 6:23
93. Jeremiah 8:20
94. Revelation 22:15
95. Matthew 5:26

be resurrected with an immortal body and inherit a place within the third kingdom.

The Disposition of Satan

If the unrighteous inherit the third kingdom, what will happen to Satan and his followers? John gave this answer:

"The devil that deceived them was cast into the lake of fire and brimstone, where the beast and the false prophet are, and shall be tormented day and night forever and ever."[96] Thus, it is evident that Satan and his followers will be cast out completely to suffer the pangs of torment for the rest of eternity.

It is not surprising to learn that false prophets will be cast out with Satan. The most treacherous enemy is the traitor within one's own camp. A false prophet concealed by the counterfeit mantle of righteousness is in a strategic position to cause grievous harm. This is why the Lord said, *"Beware of false prophets, which come to you in sheep's clothing, but inwardly they are ravening wolves."*[97]

The End

This action will ring down the final curtain on this stage of life. God the Father, with the help of His Son Jesus Christ, will now have fulfilled His promise to give His children the opportunity to experience the joys and sorrows of earth life and determine for themselves their destiny. These words recorded in the gospel of John now have deeper meaning: *"While I [Jesus] was with them in the world, I kept them in thy name: those that thou [Father] gavest me I have kept, and none of them is lost, but the son of perdition; that the scripture might be fulfilled."*[98]

---

96. Revelation 22:15
97. Matthew 7:15
98. John 17:12

These comments from Paul provide additional understanding: "*O death, where is thy sting? O grave, where is thy victory? The sting of death is sin; and the strength of sin is the law.*"[99] Death is swallowed up by the resurrection: thus the sting of death is gone.

This will be a time of great happiness for those who tried their best to follow the commandments of God. There will be a great reunion where individuals can trace their lineage back through the corridors of time to Adam and Eve. It will be a time when great, great grandfathers can meet their great, great grandchildren, when truly the hearts of the fathers and mothers will be turned to their children and the hearts of the children to their parents. It will he a time when the heart of the husband will be turned toward his wife, and the wife's toward her husband. It will be a time of appreciation, adulation, congratulations, peace, love, and joy.

But the most important time of all will occur when we, having fully realized the great importance of what has happened we will, on bended knee, acknowledge our love, awe, and gratitude to Jesus Christ, our Savior, for his willingness to be tortured to death so we could live; and, second, we will acknowledge the love and great wisdom of our Father in Heaven for establishing and executing His great plan to enable us to become all that we can be.

In summary, now that we have reviewed the great plan that God has designed for us and have examined what the scriptures say will happen after all mankind has passed beyond this mortal life, it is evident that the goal for everyone should be to strive for eternal life in the celestial kingdom. The single most important question one could possibly ask is, "What must we

---

99.1 Corinthians 15:55-56

do to obtain eternal life and qualify for entry into the celestial kingdom?"

Did God provide the answer to this question? The answer is yes! Based on the teachings of Jesus Christ, there are five critical requirements that each person must conform with in order to be saved in the celestial kingdom and inherit eternal life. These are the subjects of the next five chapters of this book.

3

The First Requirement to Qualify for Eternal Life

In the following passage John, the Beloved apostle, taught that in order to return to where God resides and obtain eternal life, we must believe or have faith in Jesus Christ. "As Moses lifted up the serpent in the wilderness, even so must the Son of man be lifted up: *that whosoever believeth in him [Christ] should not perish, but have eternal life.*"[1]

As one studies the subject of belief or faith, an interesting conflict of ideas between two apostles of Jesus Christ becomes readily apparent.

Paul, in his epistle to the Ephesians, taught: "By grace are

---
1. John 3:14-15

ye saved through faith; and that not of yourselves: it is the gift of God."[2] Did Paul mean that faith is God's gift to those persons whom He chooses to be His witnesses in the world and is bestowed immediately when a person is touched by the hand of God? If this is true, one must ask the question: Why does God give faith to some and not to others?

In contrast to Paul's comments, the apostle James taught, "Faith without works is dead."[3] Here are two apostles of Jesus Christ seemingly making statements in direct opposition to one another. Thus, the basic question now becomes: Is faith a gift from God that is given with no strings attached, or is there something we must do to qualify for this gift? Who is right, Paul or James?

This is extremely important to know, because the scriptures say that we will perish if we don't have faith in Jesus. To find the answer, it is necessary to examine these questions: What is a true saving faith and how is it developed?

Does the Bible Really Tell Us What True Faith Is?

The answer to this question is yes! Jesus said: "If ye have faith as a grain of mustard seed, ye shall say unto this mountain, Remove hence to yonder place; and it shall remove; and nothing shall be impossible unto you."[4]

How Can True Faith be Compared to a Mustard Seed?

Jesus answers this question by saying that a mustard seed is "the least of all seeds: but when it is grown, it is the greatest

---

2. Ephesians 2:8
3. James 2:20
4. Matthew 17:20

among herbs, and becometh a tree, so that the birds of the air come and lodge in the branches thereof."[5] A mustard seed does, indeed, start out as the smallest of seeds and normally grows into a giant plant that can reach a height of twelve to fifteen feet. In maturity, this mustard plant is capable of offering shade and protection from the elements to all who pass by, be they animals, birds or people.

Since Jesus compared true faith to a mustard seed, it stands to reason that, if we examine how a mustard seed can develop into a giant plant, we can determine what true faith is, how it works, and how we can obtain it.

How Is True Faith Developed?

First, in order for the mustard seed to have the best chance for growth, it must be planted in good earth. This means earth that has been prepared with the right consistency of freshly plowed soil so that essential nourishment from the soil can be transferred to the tiny seed as it grows, and thus becomes strong.

As the seed must be planted in good earth, the knowledge of God must be planted in us so our true faith can grow and become strong. This idea was taught by Jesus when he gave us the parable of the sower,[6] who went about sowing seeds by the way side, in stony places, among the thorns, and into good ground.

In explaining this parable, Jesus compared the seed to the word, or knowledge of God, and likened the ground to all mankind. When the seed is planted in good ground, it prospers and bears fruit. Likewise, when the knowledge of God is planted within a receptive person, it prospers and bears fruit. When the

---

5. See Matthew 13:32
6. Matthew 13:3-23

seed is planted in bad ground, it dies and becomes unfruitful. Similarly, when the knowledge of God is planted within a nonreceptive person, it dies and becomes unfruitful.

What exactly is the ground we must prepare within us to receive the word of God? The epistle to the Hebrews quotes the words of the Lord telling us what we must do: "1 will put my laws into their hearts, and in their minds will I write them."[7] Our *hearts* and our *minds* are the ground we must prepare to receive the word of God.

What must we do to prepare our hearts and our minds? The first requirement is to earnestly seek God: "Thou shalt find him [the Lord, thy God] if thou *seek* him with all thy heart and with all thy soul."[8] Jesus confirmed this Old 'testament passage by saying, "*Seek,* and ye shall find; *knock,* and it shall be opened unto you."[9]

How else do we seek God? Jesus said, "By prayer and fasting,"[10] prayer signifying the need to ask and fasting indicating the sincere desire to know. Prayer and fasting, then, are the necessary requirements in seeking knowledge of God.

Can we really seek God through prayer? James answers with an unqualified yes, saying, "If any of you lack wisdom, let *him ask* of God, that *giveth* to *all men* liberally, and upbraideth not; and it *shall be given him.* But let him ask in faith, nothing wavering. For he that wavereth is like a wave of the sea driven with the wind and tossed."[11] The key is to ask in faith, with an honest heart, with a real desire to know the truth.

Is anything else required in addition to prayer and fasting? In the Acts of the Apostles is found the story of Cornelius, a righteous individual, who was the first gentile to receive the

---

7. Hebrews 10:16
8. Deuteronomy 4:29
9. Luke 11:9
10. Matthew 17:21
11. James 1:5-6

THE FIRST REQUIREMENT FOR ETERNAL LIFE 59

Gospel of Jesus Christ. Learning how Cornelius prepared himself to receive the Gospel helps us to know what we must do to seek God. Cornelius was a devout man, who feared God and "gave much alms" (charitable offerings) to the people, and prayed to God always. It was the *almsgiving* that fulfilled the other requirement that prepared Cornelius to receive the Gospel. The Lord confirmed this through an angel, who told Cornelius, "Thy prayers and thine alms are come up for a memorial before God."[12]

Finally, in addition to *prayer, fasting,* and *almsgiving,* Jesus added another requirement when he taught that, unless we become like little children, we cannot enter into the kingdom of God: "Verily I say unto you, Whosoever shall not receive the kingdom of God as a little child shall in no wise enter therein."[13] What did Jesus mean? As a little child is guileless, humble, teachable, and willing and eager to learn, we also must be guileless, humble, teachable, and willing and eager to learn.

Second, once the ground *is* prepared, the seed must *be* sown.

As the seed must be sown, the knowledge of God must initially be sown in our hearts and minds so it can grow and prosper. But first, who is eligible to receive it? Again, Jesus provided the answer to this question in the parable of the sower.[14] When Jesus told us that the sower sowed seeds by the way side, in stony places, among the thorns, and, finally, into good ground, he was saying, in essence, that the knowledge of God is spread to *all* indiscriminately.

Who plants the seed of knowledge in our hearts and in our minds? This knowledge can come from other individuals,

---

12. Acts 10:4
13. Luke 18:17
14. Matthew 13:3-23

such as a friend, parents, teachers, husbands, wives. Or it can come as we read and study the word of God by any means of visual, audio, or written communication.

But who really does the initial sowing? The initial sowing of the Gospel, though it may seem to come from other people, books, and so forth, ultimately comes through the promptings of the Spirit of God. This is an important point, because to really know God, the knowledge must come from God and not man.

If this knowledge originated with man, it would be of no use. Only someone from the other side of the veil, with access to the divine plan, can really tell us what we need to do to obtain eternal life. This is evidenced in the story of Cornelius. After an angel told Cornelius that God was pleased with his prayers and almsgiving, he told Cornelius to send three men to bring the apostle Peter to him.

Prior to this time, Peter had never baptized a gentile into the Church of Jesus Christ. It was necessary for Peter to receive word from the Spirit of God that the time had now arrived for the knowledge of God (Gospel) to be taken to the gentiles. Peter did receive this word in a vision and was told to start with Cornelius.

Afterwards, "while Peter thought on the vision, the Spirit said unto him, Behold, three men seek thee. Arise therefore, and get thee down, and go with them, doubting nothing: for I have sent them."[15] In this case, Peter was used to plant the seed; however, he was motivated by the Spirit of God. Just as optimum growth required that the mustard seed be planted in the earth, so must the word be planted by the Spirit of God in our

---

15. Acts 10:19-20

mind and heart, which must be prepared through prayer, fasting, charity, and humility. This is why Paul said that true faith is one of the fruits we receive when led by the Spirit.[16]

Third, to achieve optimum growth, the mustard seed must be nourished and protected. It must receive nourishment from good soil, water, and light, and it must be protected from weeds, insects, and other elements of nature that would try to destroy it.

As the mustard seed requires nourishment and protection to achieve optimum growth, true faith requires constant nourishment and protection to achieve optimum growth. If God is going to show us how to nourish and protect our true faith, then what must we do? Our responsibility is simply to obey the will of our Father in Heaven. Jesus made this very clear by saying, "Not every one that saith unto me, Lord, Lord, shall enter into the kingdom of heaven; but he that doeth the will of my Father which is in heaven."[17]

What, specifically, must we do? Paul taught: "Put on the whole armour of God, that ye may be able to stand against the wiles of the devil....Stand therefore, having your loins girt about with truth, and having on the breast-plate of righteousness; and your feet shod with the preparations of the gospel of peace; above all, *taking the shield of faith, wherewith ye shall be able to quench all the fiery darts of the wicked.* And take the helmet of salvation, *and the sword of the Spirit,* which *is* the word of God: praying always with *all* prayer and supplication *in* the Spirit, and watching thereunto with all perseverance and supplication for all saints."[18] To be nourished and protected takes our individual effort combined with the Spirit of God. The Spirit

---

16. Galatians 5:22
17. Matthew 7:21
18. Ephesians 6:11-18

teaches us what to do. Our job is to obey and put on the whole armour of God.

Fourth, after the proper caring, watering, and weeding, the miracle eventually occurs; small leaves become visible as the tiny mustard seed takes root, begins to emerge from the ground, and push its tender leaves upward toward the sun.

As the sprouting mustard seed provides evidence that it will someday grow to be a productive plant, the seed of faith eventually blooms to provide us with the evidence that we are on the right track. But, as the mustard seed must be planted, nourished, and protected *before* it will sprout, we, in like manner, must do the will of God *before* He will provide the evidence we need to develop our faith.

Jesus said, *"If man will do his [God's] will he shall know of the doctrine, whether it be of God, or whether I speak of myself."*[19] Note the *doing comes before the confirmation.* Again, Jesus said, "He that hath my commandments, and keepeth them, he it is that loveth me: and he that loveth me shall be loved of my Father, and I will love him, and *will manifest myself to him."*[20] Observe that *obedience comes before the manifestation;* first, do the will of God, then God will provide the evidence that one is on the right track.

Fifth, though a mustard seed may sprout, it has not fulfilled its full measure of existence until it grows into a giant plant capable of offering shade and protection from the elements for all who pass by.

Nor is a person's faith developed until it grows into a vital, living testimony, capable of inspiring an individual to perfect his or her attributes of character, thus helping them to be

---

19. John 7:17
20. John 14:21

of service to others. This concept is emphasized in the parable of the sower.[21]

To make sure we did not miss the point, Jesus gave us a detailed explanation: "He that received seed into the good ground is he that *heareth the word, and understandeth it;* which *also beareth fruit,* and *bringeth forth, some an hundredfold, some sixty, some thirty.*"[22] Thus, Jesus defines "good ground" as an individual who can hear and understand the Gospel, and then carry it forth to other individuals *so* they can achieve eternal life.

In sum, the development of a true, saving faith is based on six components: hope, action, evidence, testimony, service, and motive.

To achieve a true, saving faith we must hope that God has prepared a plan for us to follow that can lead us to salvation and eternal life.[23] It is this hope that causes us to *act* to prepare our hearts and minds through prayer, fasting, charity, and humility. As soon as our hearts and minds are prepared, the Lord is ready to act through the Spirit of God to sow the seed of the Gospel within us.

As the seed begins to sprout, we become aware of the positive effect we are having on other individuals. This provides the *evidence,* hence, the knowledge, that we are on the right track toward eternal life.

As a result of this evidence comes a *testimony* that the Gospel is true.

Once this testimony is obtained, we have an obligation to *serve* by sharing the good news and by setting the example. Remember the last admonition given by the Savior just before

---

21. Matthew 13:8
22. Matthew 13:23
23. John 17:3

he ascended to heaven: "Go ye into all the world, and preach the gospel to every creature."[24]

In Galatians we find that love is the *motivation,* or underlying force, that propels an individual to fulfill the requirements to achieve a true, saving faith.[25]

It is the combination of all the above: hope, *action, evidence, testimony, service,* and *love,* repeated over and over again, that develops our faith into a true, saving faith. As each spiral of these six components is completed, a particle of faith is developed. As each particle of faith multiplies upon itself, our overall faith is enlarged, and we come one step closer to achieving a true, saving faith.

If the development of faith is similar to the development of the mustard seed, then the following questions posed at the beginning of this chapter should be easily answered!

Is True Faith a Gift from God?

Yes! because (1) the seed of faith, or initial knowledge of the Gospel, is given to us from God, and (2) the development of faith requires constant help from the Spirit of God, in conjunction with our efforts, to mature into a true, saving faith. Discard either of these elements, and it would be impossible for us to obtain a true, saving faith.

If True Faith Is a Gift from God, Then How Do We Reconcile This With the Comments Made by James When He Said Faith Without Works Is Dead?[26]

If we carefully examine this scripture, we can see that

---

24. Mark 16:15
25. Galatians. 5:6
26. See James 2:20

James was pointing out the difference between a nonsaving faith and a true, saving faith. He was pointing out that if we just stand by and watch our brothers and sisters go without food or clothing, and have the means, but do nothing to help, then we do not possess a true, saving faith. He was showing that a true, saving faith will change a person's life. In other words, if a person says he has a true, saving faith but fails to do the will of God, then no change has taken place.

James also points out that even the devils believe in God and tremble. But they do not possess a true, saving faith. If a person says, "1 believe in God," but doesn't change his life to do the will of God, then that person can never obtain a true, saving faith.[27]

What scriptural evidence is available to show that true, saving faith is developed by doing the will of God? The epistle of James states that the testing of faith produces patience.[28] For example, as we can build our muscles through exercise, faith can be developed as we work on it. James also points out that works (doing the will of God) are an absolute ingredient in the building of perfect faith: "Was not Abraham our father justified by works, when he had offered Isaac his son upon the altar? Seest thou how faith wrought [worked together] with his works, and by works was faith made perfect?"[29]

Does the Old Testament Support This Concept?

Both Moses and Isaiah encouraged us to express *hope* by seeking God with all our heart and soul.[30]

Daniel, Joel, Nehemiah and Isaiah all taught that, once we begin to seek God, *the Holy Spirit will act* to instruct us in

---

27. James 2:15-19
28. James 1:3
29. James 2:21-22
30. Deut. 4:29; Isaiah 55:6

what to do.[31] Our duty to act to obey the instructions of the Holy Spirit is outlined in Deuteronomy, Psalms, and Exodus.[32] Moses taught that, *after* we begin to do the will of God, He (God) will provide the *evidence* by manifesting His glory unto us.[33] In the book of Psalms we are instructed to place our trust in the Lord so we can receive a sure *testimony* that will make us wise.[34] Our responsibility to *serve* (by sharing the doings of the Lord) is defined in Exodus, Psalms, and Isaiah.[35] In both Deuteronomy and Leviticus we find that the primary motivation that should direct all our actions is simply the *love* of God and love for our fellowmen.[36]

In summary, a true, saving faith is the amount of faith within us that enables us to do the will of God to the level required for us to return and live in His presence after we depart this mortal life and inherit eternal life. True faith can be measured. In other words, the amount of faith a person has is in direct proportion to the effort he or she is willing to put forth to do the will of God.

It would be very difficult for one to obtain a true, saving faith immediately. It is normally developed over a long period of time and takes great effort.

God does know who will develop the necessary faith to return to His kingdom, because God knows all things. But just because God knows who will develop the required faith does not mean the individual was born with that faith. One may forecast our potential, but it can never become a reality until we achieve it through toil and suffering. For example, we know that iron has the potential to become steel; however, it can never reach that state until it goes through the required refining process.

---

31. Dan. 2:28; Neh. 9:20; Joel 2:28-29; Isaiah 11:2
32. Deut. 4:40; 6:17; 7:9; Psalms 37:3; Exodus 20:5-6
33. Leviticus 9:6
34. Psalms 34:22; 19:7
35. Exodus 9:16; Psalms 9:11; 105:1; Isaiah 43:26
36. Deut. 6:5; Leviticus 19:18

Thus, God knows who has the potential to develop the faith necessary to return to His kingdom. However, that individual can never do so until he or she goes through the refining process required to develop a true, saving faith.

The bottom line concerning why a belief in God is necessary to obtain salvation is that if a belief in God does not exist, there would be no incentive to follow His commandments. And if we do not obey the commandments, we cannot obtain eternal life.

4

The Second Requirement to Qualify for Eternal Life

In the following passage Jesus taught that unless we repent of our sins we will all perish and cannot return to where God resides: *"Except ye repent, ye shall all likewise perish."*[1]

Since, as part of our eternal progression, it is necessary for us to come to earth and be exposed to good and evil, it is only natural that we will make some mistakes. Somewhere within the plan a method had to be incorporated that would enable us to learn from these mistakes so we could change our ways and be able to continue our progression.

The question now becomes, is it possible for a person to

---

1. Luke 13: 2–3

have their sins eternally forgiven and be saved in the kingdom of God by simply praying to the Lord and verbally acknowledge that he or she is a sinner, and accept Him as their personal Savior; or is there something else we must do to qualify to have our sins forgiven? This is extremely important to know, because the scriptures say that we will perish if we don't repent.

To find the answer, we need to consider the following questions: What is the code of ethical and moral behavior established by God? What does it mean to repent? What is the process of repentance?

What Is the Code of Ethical and Moral Behavior Established by God?

To examine the ethical and moral code established by God, it is necessary to begin with the Ten Commandments listed in the Old Testament. Briefly, these are the commandments that Moses brought down from Mount Sinai that were written by the hand of God:

(1) Thou shalt have no other Gods before me. (2) Thou shalt not make [or worship] any graven image. (3) Thou shalt not take the name of the Lord thy God in vain. (4) Thou shalt remember the Sabbath day, to keep it holy. (5) Thou shalt honour thy father and thy mother. (6) Thou shalt not kill. (7) Thou shalt not commit adultery. (8) Thou shalt not steal. (9) Thou shalt not bear false witness against thy neighbor. (10) Thou shalt not covet... anything that is thy neighbor's.[2]

Approximately twelve hundred years after the Ten Com-

---

2. Exodus 20: 3–17

mandments were given, Jesus came on the scene and, expanding on the truth given in Proverbs, taught that the best way to keep from transgressing these commandments is to realize that sin originates in the mind and if one is to control his actions he needs to control his thoughts.[3]

In conformity with this truth, Jesus said, in effect, "Ye have heard it said thou shalt not kill. But I say unto you that whosoever is angry with his brother without a cause shall be in danger of the judgement.[4] Ye have heard it said thou shalt not commit adultery. But I say unto you that whosoever looketh on a woman to lust after her hath committed adultery with her already in his heart.[5] Ye have heard it said thou shalt not forswear thyself, but shalt perform unto the Lord thine oaths. But I say unto you swear not at all.[6] Ye have heard it said an eye for an eye, and a tooth for a tooth. But I say unto you whosoever shall smite thee on thy right cheek, turn to him the other also.[7] Ye have heard it said thou shalt love thy neighbor and hate thine enemy. But I say unto you love your enemies."[8]

Some time later Jesus summarized all of the commandments into just two. It was his answer to a Pharisee trained as a lawyer who tempted him with the question "which is the greatest commandment in the law?" Jesus said, "Thou shalt love the Lord thy God with all thy heart, and with all thy soul, and with all thy mind. This is the first and great commandment. And the second is like unto it, Thou shalt love thy neighbour as thyself. On these two commandments hang all the law and the prophets."[9]

Can we argue with this statement? If a person really loves God, he will keep the commandments of God, and if a person

---

3. See Proverbs 23:7
4. See Matthew 5:21-22
5. See Matthew 5:27-28
6. See Matthew 5:33–34
7. See Matthew 5:38–39
8. See Matthew 5:43–44
9. Matthew 22:35-40

really loves his neighbor, he will not want to cause him any anguish or harm. These are the code of values that are the foundation stones for building good people and great nations. This is the system of values that can help us reach toward the goal taught by Jesus when he said, "Be ye therefore perfect, even as your Father which is in heaven is perfect."[10]

What Does It Mean to Repent?

Repentance simply means to willingly change and conform one's heart and actions to a code of ethics and moral laws established by God.

What Is the Process of Repentance?

One of the best ways to show what the Bible teaches on this subject is to examine the program of a group of individuals who had to change their behavior or suffer the consequences–insanity or death. By this, we are moving from the theory of repentance into the real world of the street-wise veteran who has actually fought the battle in the trenches and returned to tell what is really required to achieve the victory.

The following information was distilled from *Alcoholics Anonymous* (Big Book),[11] *The Little Red Book*,[12] and *Getting Better Inside Alcoholics Anonymous.*[13] It is not my intent to give an in-depth review of what Alcoholics Anonymous teaches, but only an overview so the reader can appreciate the inner

---

10. Matthew 5:48
11. *Alcoholics Anonymous* (The Big Book)
    (New York: World Services, Inc. 1976), (hereafter cited as *Alcoholics Anonymous*). For additional information, write *Alcoholics Anonymous,* P.O. Box 459, Grand Central Station, New York, N.Y. 10163-1100.
12. Hazelden Foundations, *The Little Red Book* (New York: Harper and Row, rev. ed. 1987).
13. Nan Robertson (Fawcett Crest), *Getting Better Inside Alcoholics Anonymous* (New York: Ballantine Books, 1988), (hereafter cited as *Inside Alcoholics Anonymous*).

workings of this program. For further information, I recommend the reader write to the organizations listed in the footnotes and request a copy of the books described.

Alcoholics Anonymous was founded in 1935 by Bill Wilson and Dr. Bob Smith. Both individuals were alcoholics. Both had judged themselves as being beyond help, because they had tried to quit numerous times without success. It was after they had discovered the answer that both were able to overcome their addiction and begin to live a normal and happy life.

What was it that Bill Wilson and Dr. Bob found that has been instrumental in literally saving the lives of millions of people over the last fifty years? The secret lay in Twelve Steps that, when properly followed, enabled the alcoholic to become free of alcoholism. These are the steps they say a person must follow to create an honest change of behavior.

The Twelve Steps of Alcoholics Anonymous

Step 1: *They must admit that they are powerless over alcohol—that their lives have become unmanageable.*

This first step acknowledges that alcoholics are absolutely physically and mentally powerless to overcome the terrible state in which they exist. Alcohol is the master and they are the slaves. When they become slaves to the bottle, all that remains of once vibrant human beings are physical, mental, spiritual, and social wrecks. Loving relations, job, and all that is really important have been torn asunder. Life has lost all purpose and meaning. The only thing that really matters is where the next drink is coming from.

This is the state in which most alcoholics exist. They have

nothing to look forward to except insanity or an alcoholic death, and nothing will change until they come to understand the nature of their illness, are honestly willing to admit they have a problem, acknowledge that alcohol is the reason for all their troubles, and concede that they cannot get well on their own. Once they reach this point and become willing do anything to get better, that is when forward progression can start to take place.

Step 2: *They must believe that a Power greater than themselves can restore them to sanity.*

This step recognizes that compulsive drinking results in insane behavior that prevents drinkers from believing that a higher power can help them stop drinking. In actuality, this higher power is normally the only chance they have to overcome their drinking problem. So, until they are willing to believe, little progress can be made.

When A.A. first came into existence in 1935, about half of the original fellowship were either atheists (denied the existence of God) or agnostics (doubted the existence of God). It did not take long, however, for them to discover that if they could lay aside their prejudices and express a willingness to believe in a power greater than themselves, provided they took other simple steps, they were able to obtain results even though they could not fully define or comprehend the power behind the results.

Step 3: *They must make a decision to turn their will and their lives over to the care and direction of God as they understand Him.*

While Step 1 requires alcoholics to admit they are powerless over alcohol, and Step 2 requires that they believe it takes a higher power to solve their problem, this step requires them to put this belief into action, to make the effort to turn to God (as each member understands Him) and obey His will so their character defects can be corrected.

A basic, fundamental belief in A.A. is that the troubles alcoholics experience are essentially of their own making, that alcoholics are basically self-serving, self-seeking individuals who care only about themselves and the gratification of their own personal needs. They believe that they cannot overcome their problem until they learn to become less interested in themselves and more interested in others. They say that only a belief in a higher power has been able to make that truly possible:

"We decided that hereafter in this drama of life, God was going to be our director. He is the Principal; we are His agents. He is the Father; we are His children. Most good ideas are simple, and this concept was the keystone of the new and triumphant arch through which we passed to freedom."[14]

Step 4: They must make a searching and fearless moral inventory of themselves.

The purpose of this step *is to* enable alcoholics to recognize their weaknesses *so* steps *can be* taken *to* correct the faults. This inventory is a sorrowful, gut-wrenching, soul-searching ordeal, but a necessary part of the recovery process. A.A. believes that liquor is but a symptom, and the symptom cannot be cured until the root causes are uncovered and resolved.

They say that alcoholics are angry people, resentful because they perceive that their pocketbooks, ambitions, or personal relationships have been hurt or threatened by people, in-

---

14. Alcoholics Anonymous, p.62

stitutions, or principles. They discovered that, if they wanted to live a really happy life, they had to master their resentments.

Since they can never hope to control the actions of others, they are taught to look upon people who have wronged them as also being spiritually sick. Thus, when offended, they avoid retaliation by saying to themselves, "This is a sick man. How can I be helpful to him?"[15] By dismissing the wrongs of other individuals, they are now in a position to find a solution to the problems they can control. To do this, they methodically and unmercifully examine their own shortcomings, looking for signs of selfishness, self-pity, self-seeking, intolerance, belligerence, vindictiveness, dishonesty, jealousy, suspicion, false pride, criticism, and fear. By doing this they come to understand their character defects that have insulated them from both God and their fellow human beings.

Step 5. *They must admit to God, to themselves, and to another human being the exact nature of their wrongs.*

Having made a list of their character defects, this step calls for alcoholics to confess to themselves, God, and a third party (normally a trusted, properly appointed authority of a religious denomination) the exact nature of their wrongs. When this step is accomplished, it serves to demonstrate their total sincerity in being willing to do whatever is necessary to change their way of life.

They say that when they confess to a third party every dark cranny of their past, withholding nothing, then fears immediately began to fall away, self-respect starts to return, and tranquillity commences to be felt, all this bearing witness that they are on the right path, walking hand in hand with their

---

15. *Ibid.,* p.67

Creator. Conversely, they say that their experience has proven that if they do not confess all, then their forward progression is halted until this step is honestly completed.

Step 6: *They must be ready to have God remove all of their character defects.*

The purpose of this step is to encourage a mental review of the first five steps to ensure both the letter and the spirit of each step have been complied with. If they still cling to something they will not let go, they must ask God to help them resolve the deficiency. Once this is accomplished, they say they can now truly present themselves before their Creator and declare themselves ready and willing to undergo the rest of the process so the acknowledged character flaws can be removed.

Step 7: *They must humbly ask Him to remove their shortcomings.*

A.A. recognizes the need to ask God for help. This step calls for alcoholics, when they are ready, to pray and vocally ask for God's assistance in helping them overcome their problem. They are taught to say something like this:

"My Creator, I am now willing that you should have all of me, good and bad. I pray that you now remove from me every single defect of character which stands in the way of my usefulness to you and my fellows. Grant me strength, as I go out from here, to do your bidding. Amen."[16]

Step 8: *They must make a list of all persons they had harmed, and become willing to make amends to them all.*

The purpose of this step is to prepare for a plan of action that will help repair the damage done to people on the list who suffered physical, mental, or financial harm from the actions of the alcoholic. Experience has shown that few alcoholics re-

---

16. Ibid., p.76

alize that their own names head the list of those they have wronged, and by doing this they are making amends to themselves as well as others.

Step 9: *They must make direct amends to such people wherever possible, except when to do so would injure them or others.*

The easy part is to list the names of those harmed; the hard part is to reach a state of mind where one is willing to take action to make the necessary amends. This step calls for alcoholics to go to the people who have been harmed and strive to repair the damage that has occurred. A.A. members say this is necessary to qualify themselves to be of maximum service to God and the people about them. They say that alcoholics are like tornadoes roaring their way through the lives of others, breaking hearts, uprooting affections, and killing sweet relationships.

Alcoholics who see no need to change are compared to the farmer who comes up out of his basement after a cyclone has destroyed most of his house and comments how nice it is that the wind has stopped but sees no need to repair any of the damage caused by the wind. A.A. members are taught that people are more interested in a demonstration of goodwill than just talk of spiritual discoveries.

Some wrongs can never be fully righted, and alcoholics should not worry about them if they can honestly say that they would right them if they could. They are taught that if this phase is meticulously followed, they will experience new freedom, happiness, serenity, and purpose of being, and will come to realize that God is doing for them what they could not do for themselves.

Step 10: *They must continue to take a personal inventory*

and, when they are wrong, promptly admit it.

The purpose of *this* step *is to* remind alcoholics that they are never cured but are always only one *drink* away from slipping off the straight and narrow path into the prison of an alcoholic hell. Thus, while Step 4 calls for a written inventory so they can see their defects and the harm they have caused, this step calls for a daily review of this inventory so they can immediately recognize when they start to slip.

To stay on track, they are taught to immediately set right any new mistakes and continue to watch for selfishness, dishonesty, resentment, and fear. They are also urged to make amends quickly if they have harmed anyone, and continuously try to help someone who has succumbed to the same problem.

When this is done, they say, they feel as though they have been placed in a position of neutrality—safe and protected. They teach their membership that the ability to overcome is contingent on the maintenance of one's spiritual condition. Their daily goal is simply to carry the vision of God's will into all of their activities.

Step 11: *They must seek through prayer and meditation to improve their conscious contact with God as they understand Him, praying only for knowledge of His will for them and the power to carry that out.*

While Step 10 encourages the need for a continuous daily inventory, this step suggests the most effective way to accomplish this inventory. First, since God played an essential role in helping alcoholics overcome their problem, they teach that God must also play an essential role in keeping them from slipping off the straight and narrow path.

To accomplish an effective daily inventory, they teach their members that, before they retire each night, to quietly put themselves into a relaxed state of mind and then conduct a constructive mental review of all their actions that day. They are to ask themselves if they were resentful, selfish, dishonest, or afraid. Do they owe an apology? Did they keep something to themselves which should be discussed immediately with another person? Were they kind and loving toward all? What could they have done better? Were they thinking of themselves most of the time or were they thinking of what they could do for others?

They are asked to pray after this period of meditation and ask God how their actions measured up to what is expected, to know His will, and for the strength to carry out the promptings received.

When they awake in the morning, they again quietly put themselves in a relaxed state of mind and conduct a constructive mental review of what they need to accomplish that day. They are taught to conclude this period of meditation with a prayer that they be shown all through the day what their next step is to be, that they be given whatever they need to take care of such problems. They should ask especially for freedom from self-will, from self-pity, dishonest or self-seeking motives, and be careful to make no request for themselves only. Finally, as they go through the day, they should pause when agitated or doubtful and ask for the right thought or action.

Step 12: *Upon receiving a spiritual awakening as a result of these steps, they must try to carry this message to other alcoholics, and continue to practice these principles in all future personal affairs.*

This step does not merely suggest, but boldly announces

to the world that every member reaching this step has received a spiritual conviction and conversion that this program works. They now dauntlessly testify that they have tried it, it works, and that it was a higher power that helped them do it. What proof do they offer? They simply say experience is the proof. Those who accept and try to live all of the Twelve Steps seldom fail in A.A., while those who skip the spiritual principles seldom succeed.

The second part of this step proclaims their commitment to carry this message to other alcoholics. They want to carry this message for four reasons: (1) sense of duty, (2) it's pleasurable, (3) in so doing they are paying their debt to the person who took time to pass it on to them, and (4) every time they do it they take out a little more insurance for themselves against a possible slip.

They proclaim the story of A.A. by phoning, speaking, writing, handing out literature, manning duty stations, and providing funding to further the cause. In their search for prospects they contact doctors, clergy, judges, police officials, and industrial personnel.

Once they find a prospect, the message they leave is simple. They tell of their own experience, the trouble liquor has caused in their life, and how hopeless the life of an alcoholic really is. They explain the insidious nature of the disease and that many people are already doomed and just don't realize it. They openly tell how it takes a higher power than themselves to overcome their problem.

They tell their prospects that if they will diligently conduct a severe housecleaning of their alcoholic past, work hand in hand with this higher power, and labor for the welfare of others instead of themselves, they can expect a sober, happy, and purposeful life. They acknowledge that all will not be sunshine and roses, that there are periods of darkness, but no matter how dark the night, a beautiful dawn is just around the corner.

So these are the Twelve Steps considered by A.A. to be the answer in helping its members overcome their dependency upon alcohol. But what does all this have to do with repentance?

The Twelve Steps bear a striking resemblance to the New Testament step-by-step process for changing so-called "sinful behavior." Bill Wilson, one of the founders of AA, who originally documented the Twelve Steps in his book, *Alcoholics Anonymous,* often stated there was nothing original about the Twelve Steps. He said they were grounded in first-century Christianity. It was the teachings of an organization called the Oxford Group that helped him overcome his drinking problem in 1935.

Interestingly, this group received its name because, when it was formed in 1921, it was made up mostly of undergraduates at Christ Church, a college of Oxford University, and was initially known as a nondenominational First Century Christian Fellowship. But the more one studies the origin of these Twelve Steps, the more one comes to realize that they are not only taught in the New Testament, but in the Old Testament as well.

When a comparison is made between Rabbenau Yonah of Gerona's "Sixteen Principles" listed in his *Gates of Repentance*[17] and the Twelve Steps of Alcoholics Anonymous, one cannot help but *be* impressed with the striking similarities. What

---

17. Shaarei Teshuvah, *The Gates of Repentance*, by Yonoh Ben Avraham of Gerona, trans. Shraga Silverstein (New York; Jerusalem: Feldheim Publishers, 1967). Sole sales agcy, Philipp Feldheim, Inc. "The House of the Jewish Book," 96 E Bdwy, New York, 10002.

is evident from this comparison *is* that Jewish step-by-step teaching concerning how to change sinful behavior is very similar to the A.A. Twelve Step process for changing addictive behavior.

Scriptural Correlation Between the Twelve Steps and Both the Old Testament and New Testament

Step 1: *Admit Powerless to Control Problem.*

Old Testament: In Psalms 38 we find the admonition to declare our iniquity and feel sorrow for our sins.[18]

New Testament: In 1 John we find the promise that if we will confess our sins, the Lord will forgive us and cleanse us from all unrighteousness.[19]

Step 2: *Admit Need for Help from Higher Power.*

Old Testament: 2 Chronicles teaches that if we will believe *in* God and His prophets we will prosper.[20]

New Testament: Jesus taught that all things are possible for him that believes in God.[21]

Step 3: *Make Decision to Turn Problems Over to God.*

Old Testament: The Psalmist instructs us to commit our lives to the Lord and put our trust in Him.[22]

New Testament: The Apostle Paul taught that we should *be in* subjection (turn our lives over) to the Father of our spirit and live.[23]

Step 4: *Make inventory of Character Faults.*

Old Testament: Psalm 38 vividly describes the moral inventory David went through before he felt worthy to ask for help from God.[24]

New Testament: In Paul's letter to Timothy we find the

---

18. Psalms 38:18
19. See 1 John 1:9
20. See 2 Chron. 20:20
21. See Mark 9:23;10:27
22. See Psalms 37:5
23. See Heb. 12:9
24. See Psalms 38:1-22

advice to meditate upon our moral character traits so our improvement may appear to all.[25] And Paul also mentions, in his letter to the Corinthians, that godly sorrow is good, because "It worketh repentance to salvation."[26]

Step 5: *Confess Faults to Another Person.*

Old Testament: The advice given in Proverbs is that those who confess and forsake their sins shall have mercy.[27]

New Testament: The same advice was given by James when he taught that we need to confess our faults one to another so we can be healed.[28]

Step 6: *Analyze Eligibility for Divine Assistance by Reviewing the Previous Steps for Compliance.*

Old Testament: Proverbs teaches us to ponder the direction we are going to ensure we are established on the straight and narrow path.[29]

New Testament: Paul cautions, in his letter to Timothy, to continue to review (by taking heed unto) the direction in which we are headed so that we can save ourselves and others.[30]

Step 7: *Ask God for Help.*

Old Testament: From Proverbs comes the promise that if we will acknowledge the Lord in all our ways, He will direct our path.[31]

New Testament: In the Sermon on the Mount, Jesus taught of the need to ask God for the good things we need.[32]

Step 8: *Make List of People Injured by One's Actions.*

Old Testament: The prophet Jeremiah taught the need to amend our ways as we turn from evil.[33]

New Testament: Jesus taught that before we approach God we need to first make reconciliation to the people we have harmed.[34]

---

25. See 1 Tim. 4:15
26. See 2 Cor. 7:9–10
27. See Prov. 28:13
28. See James 5:16
29. See Prov. 4:26
30. See Tim. 4:16
31. See Prov. 3:6
32. See Matt. 7:7
33. See Jer. 35:15
34. See Matt. 5:23-24

Step 9: *Make Direct Amends to the Injured Parties Where Possible.*

Old Testament: The prophet Ezekiel also taught the need to restore (whenever possible) the damages caused by sinful behavior.[35]

New Testament: In his conversation with Zacchaeus, Jesus taught that the reward of salvation is tied directly to the effort one puts forth to restore any damages caused by inappropriate behavior.[36]

Step 10: *Continue to Review Previous Steps for Compliance and Rectify Any Slippage Immediately.*

Old Testament: The book of Job vividly describes the efforts Job put forth in holding fast to living a righteous life.[37]

New Testament: Paul taught of the need to remain steadfast in trying to resolve wrongs so that our labor will not be in vain.[38]

Step 11: *Continue to Magnify the Relationship with God Through Meditation and Prayer.*

Old Testament: The prophet Nahum taught of the need to continually watch the way, strengthen our loins, and fortify our power.[39] And Joel said that whosoever will call upon the name of the Lord will be delivered.[40]

New Testament: Jesus taught the need to establish an ongoing daily program of watching and praying that we may be accounted worthy to return to God.[41]

Step 12: *Help Others in the Same Situation.*

Old Testament: The prophet Isaiah also taught the importance of everyone helping his neighbours.[42]

New Testament: Jesus taught that, once we have received the

---

35. Ezek. 33:15–16
36. See Luke 19:8–9
37. See Job 27:5–6
38. See 1 Cor. 15:58
39. See Nahum 2:1
40. See Joel 2:32
41. See Luke 21:36
42. See Isa.. 41:6-7

help we needed, we now have a responsibility to strengthen others, through service and proper example.[43]

What Can We Learn from the Experience of Alcoholics Anonymous?

The steps that help the alcoholic overcome his addictive behavior are, in essence, the same steps taught in both the Old and New Testaments to help one overcome sinful behavior. Knowing this helps us to understand the following insights into God's plan.

As There is Hope for the Alcoholic to Achieve Complete Recovery, There is Hope for the Individual Burdened with Sin to Achieve Complete Redemption

When some individuals begin their spiral descent into the world of alcoholism, all things near and dear slowly lose their importance until the only thing that really matters is where the next drink is coming from. Normally, a person is not willing to turn to A.A. until he has reached rock bottom.

During the early years, members of A.A. felt that if a person was still married, with a wife and children living at home, and did not have money problems, he was probably not desperate enough to be helped; he had not lost enough to have hit rock bottom. When some alcoholics are desperate enough to give up family, friends, home, and job for a drink, they can represent almost a worst case situation when it comes to addictive behavior.

But, in the world of A.A., experience has proven that as soon as these types of alcoholics are willing to follow the Twelve

---

43. See Luke 22:32; John 13:14-15; Matt. 5:16

Steps, immediate help is available from a higher power. Therefore, if these Twelve Steps can help an alcoholic of this type, then it gives hope to the world that these same principles can help anyone overcome even the most addictive, sinful behavior.

As the Alcoholic Must Put Forth Effort to Win the Battle, Effort Is Likewise Required of Those Burdened With Sin to Achieve the Victory

One of the most important lessons learned from the A.A. program is that effort is required to change addictive behavior. Bill Wilson often mentioned that if an alcoholic failed to perfect and enlarge his spiritual life through work and self-sacrifice for others, he could not survive the certain trials and low spots ahead.

Whenever Bill would reflect upon the events that helped him to overcome his drinking habit, he would tell of the many times he had gone to his old hospital in despair, then, after talking to an alcoholic there, he would be amazingly lifted up and set on his feet. It was this experience that solidified Bill's belief that, when all other measures failed, work and helping another alcoholic would save the day.

Since the same steps for overcoming alcoholic addictive behavior are also applicable in overcoming sinful behavior, it then follows that effort is also required. One should note that, of the Twelve Steps, at least four require the expenditure of physical effort.

This gives us the answer to the question put forth at the beginning of this chapter regarding the "acceptance only" philosophy: "Can a person simply pray to the Lord, accept Him as his personal Savior, and verbally acknowledge that he is a sinner, and do nothing more, and then have all his sins forgiven and be saved in the kingdom of God?"

Experience garnered in A.A. indicates that one can only expect help from God as long as one is willing to put forth the effort to qualify for that help. The grace is there, but we have to exercise the effort to qualify for that grace. The perfection of man requires work, effort, sweat, perseverance, and sacrifice.

As God Can Help the Alcoholic Escape from the Captivity of the Effects of Alcohol, in Similar Fashion He Can Free Anyone Chained Down by the Effects of Sinful Behavior

Some years ago a friend of mine was working in a brewery on the west coast. His wife had passed away a few years before, and to pass the lonely hours he would carry a six pack or two home with him after work. After a light supper he would sit down, turn on the television, and for the next several hours drink himself into an alcoholic daze. Around ten o'clock he would make his way into the bedroom and collapse into bed. This became a standard routine, and as the years went by, his periods of depression worsened.

One day his depression became so great he felt he would be better off dead. While contemplating this thought, he remembered some advice he had once received. "When all else fails, God will help. All you need to do is ask."

With this thought in mind, he went to his bedroom, knelt

down, and offered up a simple prayer. "Please, God, I'm an alcoholic, I've tried to quit but I just can't. Please help me!" He rose from his knees and climbed into bed. Just before turning off the light, he checked his radio to make sure it was on and tuned to a local station that played easy listening music all night. Over the years he had used this type of music to help him go to sleep.

At approximately two o'clock he awoke from deep slumber. Coming over the radio was a commercial for Alcoholics Anonymous. Groggily, he searched for a pencil to write down the phone number. Too late! The commercial was over and still no pencil.

The next night, having completely forgotten the previous night's experience, he went to bed at ten o'clock. At two o'clock he again awoke with a start. Again, the same commercial began to air. Again, my friend scrambled for something to write down the phone number, and again he was too late.

The third night, having recalled his prayer and the events of the previous two nights, before retiring, he placed a pencil and some paper within easy reach. When 2:00 a.m. arrived, a familiar scene began to unfold. Only now, with pencil in hand, he wrote the long sought telephone number. The next morning he dialed the number, a friendly voice responded, and a prayer was answered.

In less than a year my friend was able to conquer his dependency on alcohol, and his loneliness and depression disappeared. He found many new friends, especially the One he now prays to every night with a thankful heart.

And what about those commercials? My friend stated that, in all the years he had gone to bed listening to that particular radio station, the only time he ever heard that commercial played was during the three days when the incident occurred. He had never heard it before the incident, and afterward, he never heard it again.

What happened in this case is what A.A. likes to refer to as a spiritual awakening. Some members experience it quickly, as in the incident described. For others, their awakening is progressive, in which each step plays a part. But, regardless of whether the impact is sudden and profound or just comes gradually, the important point is that it will come.

Can God free anyone chained down from the effects of sinful behavior, as He can help the alcoholic escape from the captivity of alcoholism? Isaiah writes: "Let us reason together, saith the Lord: Though your sins be as scarlet, they shall be as white as snow."[44]

As the Evidence of God's Help Will Be Obvious to the Recovered Alcoholic, His Hand Will Also Be Visibly Manifested to the Soul Who Is Striving to Complete the Repentance Process

Alcoholics Anonymous began in 1935 with two members. By 1988 there were almost two million members in 63,000 groups in 114 countries around the world, and the numbers are doubling every ten years.[45] This means that the program of AA is working for all types of individuals, regardless of nationality or race.

This, in turn, means that these same principles will help a person from any race or nationality. As the alcoholic can expect this support, so can one trying to overcome sinful behav-

---
44. Isaiah 1:18
45. *Inside Alcoholics Anonymous, p.74*

ior, regardless of current religious beliefs. The great plan devised by our Father in Heaven is available to everyone.

As a Testimony Will Grow in the Heart of the Alcoholic from the Evidence Revealed, a Testimony Will Blossom in the Hearts of Those Who Have Changed Their lives from Sinful Pursuits by the Manifestation of the Hand of God

As mentioned previously, when A.A. first came into existence in 1935, about half of the original fellowship were either atheists or agnostics, priding themselves on their ability to make do using their own resourcefulness. They saw no need to place their trust in or conform their actions to any so—called expectations of a higher power.

When someone of this persuasion has to suddenly declare his philosophy of life wrong, it completely goes against the grain and is a bitter pill to swallow.

Bill Wilson said that, for this group, it took the self imposed crisis of alcoholism to show that they could not postpone or evade, but had to fearlessly face, the proposition that God was a reality and had the power to help them overcome their problem.

He said that if a mere code of morals or better philosophy of life was sufficient to solve their problem, they would have readily accepted it rather than give in and turn to God. But they found that no such code or philosophy would work, no matter how hard they tried.

In short, if there was any one group living on earth who did not want to believe in God, it was this group of atheists and agnostics that comprised over fifty percent of the original fellowship of A.A. But it was this group who discovered that, not until they obtained a belief in God and were willing to follow the Twelve Steps, were they able to receive the help needed to overcome their problem. In doing so, they found something more precious than they had ever known before—peace of mind and purpose to life.

From this information it is reasonable to believe that, as God is indispensable in helping agnostics and atheists surmount their drinking problem, He is equally indispensable in helping anyone overcome sinful behavior.

As the Recovered Alcoholic, in Appreciation, Feels the Need to Give Service to Others with Similar Needs, the Individual Who Has Been Cleansed from Sin also Senses a Responsibility to Help Others in the Same Situation

An experience of Bill W. in the hospital gives us some important insights into the workings of God. As Bill was lying in his hospital bed making a fervent petition to overcome his addiction to alcohol, he received a remarkable manifestation.

He describes what happened: "The effect was 'electric'... There was a sense of victory, followed by such a peace and serenity as I had never known. There was utter confidence. I felt lifted up, as though the great clean wind of a mountaintop blew through and through. God comes to most men gradually, but His impact on me was sudden and profound." He cried out, "If there be a God, let Him show Himself!"

He then told how the room blazed with light, and how he

was filled with a "joy beyond description," followed by a desire to help others experience the same things.[46]

Analyzing what happened to Bill helps us gain some understanding of the workings of God. What Bill felt that day was a power with five distinct effects: (1) A feeling of being cleansed as his torment was swept away. (2) A feeling that victory was possible, as despondency was replaced with confidence. (3) A feeling of joy beyond description. (4) A desire to help others experience what he had. (5) The feeling that what he had been given was given freely.

This experience demonstrates two important insights:

First, the ultimate goal of the great plan of God is to perfect mankind to the greatest extent possible, and do it by urging each of us to help our fellowmen. This idea is one of the central messages in the gospel of John and can be illustrated by the following incident.

The night before Jesus was crucified, he had a last supper with his disciples. Knowing he was going to die the next day, he used this last opportunity to teach his disciples an important concept. When Jesus finished his supper, he poured some water into a basin and began to wash the disciples' feet and wipe them with a towel. Peter was astonished at this and forbade the Savior to wash his feet. Jesus answered that if he was not allowed to wash Peter's feet, then Peter could not be a disciple.

The Savior then explained to the apostles that he had given them an example, that as he had served them, they, in turn, should serve their fellowmen.[47]

The second point to be gleaned from Bill's experience in the hospital regards the motivational factor associated with the

---

46. *Alcoholics Anonymous,* p.14
47. John 13:4-15

giving of service. The feeling Bill Wilson described was what John tells us is the perfect love of God. He says that it is only this kind of love that can cast out fear and torment.[48] Paul tells us that God's perfect love is the greatest gift one can receive and gives it the special name "charity." "And above all these things, put on charity, which is the bond of perfectness. And let the peace of God rule in your hearts."[49] Thus, as love (charity) is the motivating power than enables an alcoholic to achieve complete recovery, so is love (charity) the motivating power that enables an individual burdened with the effects of sin to be cleansed so progression can continue.

Where Specifically Did This Power (Charity) Come From?

The psalmist David acknowledges that God is the only one who has the power to create a clean heart and renew a right spirit within us.[50] But the New Testament gives more specific information as to who, specifically, can accomplish this cleansing action. 1 John teaches that there is only one individual who has the power to "cleanse us from all unrighteousness,"[51] and that person is Jesus Christ. Thus, in a sense, this power is "bestowed upon" Christ's righteous followers. Its source, like all other blessings of the Atonement, is the grace of God.

What Are the Characteristics of Charity?

In 1 Corinthians, Paul outlines some attributes of charity that might correspond to this list of modern terms: stamina, kindness, tolerance, humility, unpretentiousness, respectabil-

---

48. See 1 John 4:18
49. See Colossians 3:14–15
50. See Psalms 51:10
51. See 1 John 1:9

ity, selflessness, calmness, virtue, integrity, truthfulness, willpower, trust, endurance, and peace of mind.[52] These are the same characteristics that many alcoholics admit to having developed in overcoming such ingrained attitudes as selfishness, self-pity, self-seeking, intolerance, belligerence, vindictiveness, dishonesty, jealousy, suspicion, false pride, criticism, and fear.

How Does One Obtain True Charity?

As proven in A.A., the only requirement necessary is a willingness to yield one's heart to God and obey the Twelve Steps with honest intent. God has said, "Behold, I stand at the door, and knock: if any man hear my voice, and open the door, I will come into him, and will sup with him, and he with me."[53]

What Role Do We Play in Offering True Charity to Others?

When Bill Wilson and Dr. Bob Smith founded A.A., they knew that serving others was one of the most important steps in helping an alcoholic overcome his drinking habit. But they discovered that just serving others was not enough. The key that made the difference between success and failure was in how the service was given.

They found that the minute they put their work on a service plane, the alcoholic began to rely upon their assistance rather than upon God. If their service was spent just trying to meet the material needs of the alcoholic rather than helping him develop a personal relationship in God, then the alcoholic would just clamor for more material help by claiming he could

---

52. See 1 Corinthians 13:4–8
53. See Revelation 3:20

not master alcohol until all his material needs were cared for.

Bill declared that an alcoholic cannot stop drinking until he learns to place his dependence on God rather that on other people.[54]

This gives us an important clue as to how to help others through true charity. In many cases we look upon charity as simply providing gifts of money or showing kindness or compassion to others. Hence, we more or less define charity as reaching out to help others in distress. Certainly, this is a form of charity, but not necessarily true charity. True charity is much more than this. The primary role we should play in offering true charity is to reach out and help others reach up so they can establish their own personal relationship with God.

In AA, some individuals just cannot accept the idea of God as being the source of providing the help they need, so they look upon their fellow members as being the higher, greater power. One of the problems this concept presents is this: Though a person is filled with the pure love of Christ, his ability to imbue others with this pure love is extremely limited. We reflect the pure love of Christ much the same way the moon reflects the light of the sun. On a dark night the light of the moon can provide some assistance in helping someone navigate to a destination, but if the traveler wants the ultimate assurance of being able to see where he is going, he must travel by the light of the sun.

One member of A.A. said he was able to quit drinking after completing Step Four but was not happy about it; it was only when he continued to progress through the Twelve Steps that he found the happiness and peace of mind he was looking

---

54. *Alcoholics* Anonymous p.98

for.[55] This individual had never established a personal relationship with God. Only after he continued through the Twelve Steps was he able to reach up and make contact and receive the serenity and peace of mind that he was seeking.

When one is filled with true charity, he will practice all lesser forms of charity. He will want to help clothe the needy, comfort the sick, and feed the poor, not merely because he thinks he should, but because that is the kind of person he has now become. However, the ultimate purpose of true charity is to help our fellowmen become like Christ, and in so doing we become more Christlike ourselves.

How Critical Is Our Participation in Helping Others Receive True Charity?

The whole concept of A.A. is built around the need for its members to reach out and help their fellowmen. They have found that, in many cases, they are the only ones who can make contact, because they have experienced the same problems themselves. They truly understand the needs of an alcoholic and can relate to him. The alcoholic can, in turn, relate to the member giving service.

In the same context, God needs our help because, in many cases, we are the only ones who can contact certain types of people. Hence, our role in spreading true charity is indispensable.

As mentioned previously, God has said that He is standing at the door knocking. Note that God will not open the door and walk in. The individual must open the door and let Him in.

---

55. *Little Red Book,* pp. 119-120

Our job is to convince people that God is out there and to open the door and let Him help them.

How Can We Be Most Effective in Helping Others Receive True Charity?

When the founders of A.A. initially established their program, they realized that, if it were to be effective, it had to function on certain basic truths or principles: (1) the service had to be free, (2) it had to be given in an unselfish manner, (3) with as much anonymity as possible, (4) with knowledge and wisdom, and finally, (5) the giver needs to walk the way he talks. They felt strongly that their membership should serve others simply because it was the right thing to do without thought of any reward.

To accomplish this, they built the following safeguards into their organization.

First, they have no fees or dues. The only requirement for membership is an honest desire to stop drinking. A.A. is not in business to make money. It owns no property, will not accept money from outsiders, and it has limited donations from its own members to a maximum of $1,000 in any one year. The only money it receives comes from member donations and profits from the six books, several booklets, and some forty-odd pamphlets it publishes each year.[56]

Next, they constantly stress the need to serve in a selfless manner. Members are admonished to think about what they can bring to a situation, not what they can get out of it. It is made clear to prospective members that A.A.'s only concern is to help the individual escape his own difficulties, and that he is

---

56. *Inside Alcoholics Anonymous*, pp. 85–87

under no obligation to return any kind of favor. It is also emphasized that a kindly act once in a while isn't enough. To be really effective, members need to act the Good Samaritan every day, even though it may not be convenient at the moment.

The concept of anonymity is another safeguard. In A.A. only first names are used, with the first initial of the last name. For example, Bill Wilson is normally referred to as Bill W. When service is given, not only is recompense not expected, but the person receiving the service may seldom know the full name of the individual dispensing it. As part of this anonymity concept, the membership is encouraged to avoid any type of limelight that might give even the appearance of a self serving motive. In keeping with this philosophy, Bill Wilson turned down a Yale doctorate of laws offered in 1954 and a cover article on him proposed by *Time* magazine.[57]

How important is knowledge and the ability to use that knowledge? Bob Smith claims it was Bill Wilson's knowledge and wisdom that played the critical role in convincing him to enter the program. Bob said that Bill W. "was the first living human with whom I had ever talked with, who knew what he was talking about in regards to alcoholism from actual experience. In other words he talked my language. He knew all the answers."[58]

The final concept AA incorporates into their program is the need to serve by example. Bill Wilson was encouraged to try the program primarily because a friend had set the example. Bob Smith, cofounder of A.A., was willing to try the program primarily because Bill Wilson had led the way. Thus, A.A. is critically aware of the need for its membership to walk the

---

57. *Inside Alcoholics Anonymous,* p.69
58. Alcoholics Anonymous, p.180

way they talk when promoting the attributes of their program to other individuals.

The principles by which A.A. regulates its program are the same principles taught in the Bible to regulate the teaching of true gospel principles. To effectively help others receive true charity, we need to conduct our actions in much the same manner as exemplified by A.A. For example, the idea that the Gospel is to be preached freely, without charge, is found in Isaiah.[59]

In the gospel of Luke the followers of Christ are taught that, if they want to be saved in the kingdom of God, they need to lose their life in selfless service to others.[60]

The need to retain as much anonymity as possible when serving others is declared in the gospel of Matthew.[61] To accomplish this we need to learn true principles as mentioned in John,[62] then obtain the wisdom to know how to apply these true principles, as discussed in Proverbs.[63]

Finally, the need to teach by example was taught by Jesus in the gospel of John: "I have given you an example, that ye should do as I have done to you."[64]

These are the basic principles concerning the dissemination of true charity. The more one conforms to these basic principles, or truths, the more effective one can be in touching the lives of others.

Charity Is the Welding Process

Because of the tremendous growth A.A. has experienced over the years, many people have been left scratching their heads trying to explain what would account for such success. Some have speculated that it is simply the result of a bonding

---

59. See Isaiah 52:3; Micah 3:11-12; 1 Corinthians 9:18
60. See Luke 17:33
61. See Matthew 6:1,3; 8:4
62. See John 8:32
63. Proverbs 4:7
64. John 13:15

together by the common effects of a great cause. They say that, as the recovered alcoholic maintains his own sobriety, he soon becomes a physician to the next new applicant, thus creating an ever expanding chain reaction of liberation, with patients welded together by bonds of common suffering, common understanding, and stimulating action in a great cause.[65] It is true that a physician/patient welding process does occur, but not in the manner described above.

To understand the welding process, it is necessary to examine one last phenomenon experienced by many AA members who have completed the Twelve Step process. Not only have these individuals been able to overcome their alcohol problem, but many report that they have found something of much greater value.

In attempting to describe what they have found, they use such terms as purpose of life, meaning to life, sense of accomplishment, inner satisfaction, peace, serenity, utter confidence, lifted up, wonderful sense of satisfaction and well being, sense of being in control, state of exaltation, and sense of victory. They know something wonderful has occurred in their lives but find it difficult to describe what has happened.

Many have stated that the feelings they experienced were so strong it left them with a sense of wonder and gratitude, concern for others, and an entirely new outlook on life's true values.

What did happen? It is critical that we explore this question, because it helps us to truly understand the bottom line in the great plan God has for us.

When a person becomes involved in the process of giving

---

65. *Inside Alcoholics Anonymous*, p.76

true charity, one becomes part of what might be called a "triangle of joy and affection." The principle players in the triangle of affection are God, the servant, and the prospect. In this case the servant is the person who works on God's behalf to make the initial contact with the prospect. The prospect is the person who receives the help God would like him to have.

This is how the triangle works in A.A.: (1) The first side of the triangle materializes as the servant of God initiates the process by extending his hand of charity to the prospect by encouraging him to start the Twelve Step process. (2) The prospect accepts the invitation from the servant, yields his heart to God, and begins to live the Twelve Step program. (3) God extends His hand of charity to the prospect to help him overcome his problem. (4) A bond of affection develops between the prospect and God. The prospect experiences joy as love from God fills his being, and his love for God continues to grow. (5) The second side of the triangle takes shape when, as a result of Step 4, a bond of affection also begins to develop between the prospect and the servant. (6) The third side of the triangle develops when the bond of affection grows between God and the servant because of the work the servant accomplished in bringing the prospect to God.

As each new prospect is converted, new triangles of affection are created as the converted prospect reaches out to help others in need, thus creating an ever expanding chain of people welded together in triangles of affection and a great cause.

The bottom line is this: the purpose of the great plan of God is to bond together into triangles of affection and joy all of mankind who are willing. God wants us to have eternal happiness. But how happy would we be if the only individuals who really cared for us, after we return to heaven, are God the Father and Jesus Christ? The divine plan is geared to draw us all together as a total heavenly family unit, so we can enjoy the love and friendship of one another and, therefore, have the happiness that would otherwise be lost if it were not for God's divine plan.

It becomes readily apparent that love (charity) is the catalyst in accomplishing this task. It is the underpinning of God's great plan, making it possible for man to progress and become as nearly Godlike as he is willing to be. Charity is as important to God's plan as oxygen is to mortals living on earth. Because of this, it was necessary to build the entire plan around it. Without it, the plan would disintegrate as quickly as a universe would disintegrate if all gravitational force were suddenly shut off.

In summary, it does not appear that it is possible for individuals to simply pray to the Lord, accept Him as their personal Savior, verbally acknowledge that they are sinners, do nothing more, and then have all their sins forgiven and be saved in the kingdom of God.

The only way a person can accept and receive the atonement of the Savior is by sincere repentance of past transgressions and future obedience to the will of God. If sincere repentance (honest change of behavior) does not occur, then forgiveness of sin cannot take place. This is the whole crux of the plan. If a person, belabored by the effects of a guilt-ridden existence, believes in the "acceptance only" philosophy and just verbally accepts Jesus Christ as his or her personal Savior and does nothing more, then their negative behavior will never change; hence, forgiveness of sin cannot take place, and the pain caused by that behavior cannot be removed.

The individual is likely to say, "I've tried the God approach, and it didn't work; therefore, I would be better off to just give up and take my own life." In one year, over 30,000 adults and 6,000 teens in the United States committed suicide. Many of these individuals were burdened with moral transgressions and just felt life was not worth living.

To properly repent of our mistakes, we must follow certain procedures prescribed by God. To accomplish these procedures requires effort on our part and assistance from God. The procedures we must follow are these:

(1) Declare our iniquity and feel sorrow for our sins. (2) Believe that God can help us. (3) Make the decision to ask God for help. (4) Make an inventory of our character faults. (5) Confess our faults to another person. (6) Analyze eligibility for Divine assistance by reviewing the previous steps for compliance. (7) Ask God for help. (8) Make a list of people injured by our actions. (9) Make direct amends to the injured parties where possible. (10) Continue to review previous steps for compliance and rectify any slippage immediately. (11) Continue to magnify our relationship with God through meditation and prayer. (12) Help others in the same situation.

Step 12 is the most critical step. If we are to surmount the deficiency in our character that led to violations of commandments of God, we need to help others in the same situation. This is important, because helping others will help us to stay on track. This is probably why James said, "Let him know, that he which converteth the sinner from the error of his way shall save a soul from death, and shall hide a multitude of sins."[66]

Any belief that mankind does not have to go through a repentance process to correct character deficiencies that result in the violation of one of the commandments of God is at odds with what the Bible really teaches on this subject.

These steps, if followed correctly, will help anyone, regardless of race, nationality, or religion, overcome any and all sinful, addictive behavior. This is why repentance is listed as essential if one expects to reside with Jesus Christ and God the Father in the kingdom of God.

With this in mind, one could better appreciate the thought expressed by Robert Louis Stevenson: "To be what we are, and to become what we are capable of becoming is the only end of life."

---

66. James 5:20

5

The Third Requirement *to Qualify for Eternal Life*

Jesus taught that we must be baptized to be saved. "He that believeth *and is baptized shall be saved:* but he that believeth not shall be damned."[1]

When Jesus said, "he that believeth not shall be damned," notice that Jesus mentions the word "believeth" twice, but the word "baptized" is mentioned only once. Does this mean that baptism is not really necessary, that all we have to do to be saved is to believe that Jesus is the Christ? This is important to know, because if we have to be baptized to be saved, then we cannot make it into the kingdom of heaven if we don't abide by this commandment.

---

1. Mark 16:16

To find the answer we need to examine the following questions. How important is the principle of baptism? What is the meaning of baptism? What is the baptismal process? If baptism is a requirement to be saved, what will happen to all the people who have died without the opportunity to be baptized? And if baptism is so critical, why was it not recorded in the Old Testament as being performed in those days—or was it?

How Important Is the Principle of Baptism?

There are five incidents recorded in the Bible that help us answer this question.

First, Jesus, the only perfect man to ever live on the face of the earth, was baptized to fulfill all righteousness and to set the example for us to follow.[2] Matthew confirms this in his record of what happened when Jesus came to where John the Baptist was baptizing some of his followers. "Then cometh Jesus from Galilee to Jordan unto John, to be baptized of him. But John forbad him, saying, I have need to be *baptized* of thee, and comest thou to me? And Jesus answering said unto him, Suffer it to be so now: for thus it becometh us to *fulfill all righteousness.* Then he suffered him. And Jesus, when he was baptized, went up straightway out of the water: and, lo, the heavens were opened unto him, and he saw the Spirit of God descending like a dove, and lighting upon him: and lo a voice from heaven, saying, This is my beloved Son, in whom I am well pleased."[3] If it was necessary for Jesus, who did no sin, to be baptized to fulfill all righteousness, how much more important is it for us to follow his example by being baptized to fulfill all righteousness?

The *second* incident involves the conversion of Paul. Paul

---
2. See 1 Peter 2:21
3. Matthew 3:13-17

THE THIRD REQUIREMENT FOR ETERNAL LIFE

was a Pharisee working in cooperation with the high priests to persecute the followers of Jesus. One day, on the road to Damascus, the Lord appeared to Paul and asked him why he was persecuting him. Paul responded by asking the Lord what he should do. The Lord told Paul to go to Damascus and there he would receive further direction.

As a result of this encounter, Paul lost his sight. His friends led him by the hand into Damascus. Upon arriving, Paul was directed to a righteous individual named Ananias. Ananias told Paul he had been chosen to bring people to the Lord.

Some would say that a personal visitation by the Lord is all that is required to be a disciple of Christ. But that is not what happened to Paul. After Ananias restored Paul's sight, he told him to immediately go and be baptized.[4] If baptism was not necessary, why did the Lord direct Paul to Ananias to be baptized?

The *third* incident, recorded by Luke, tells how Paul was miraculously delivered from the jail of Philippi. In this account we learn that Paul and Silas were cast into prison for preaching the Gospel. At midnight an earthquake opened the prison doors and loosed the prisoners' bands. The jailor, thinking the authorities would kill him because he had allowed his prisoners to escape, was ready to commit suicide when, suddenly, Paul called out to inform the jailor that they were still there.

The integrity Paul and Silas displayed so impressed the jailor that he came to them and asked, "Sirs, what must I do to be saved? And they (Paul and Silas) said, Believe on the Lord Jesus Christ, and thou shalt be saved, and thy house."[5] What happened next is very important: "And he [the jailor]... was

---

4. See Acts 3:18
5. Acts 16:30-31

baptized, and all his [family], straightway."⁶

So here you have the jailor and his family believing and accepting the gospel; yet, even though it is the middle of the night, Paul still takes the time to baptize each member of the family. Why would Paul have done this if baptism was not absolutely necessary?

The *fourth* incident occurred on the day of Pentecost. On this day Peter had been preaching to a large gathering of people. When he had finished, the crowd of listeners, having accepted his teachings, asked: "What shall we do? Then Peter said unto them, Repent, and be *baptized* every one of you in the name of Jesus Christ for the remission of sins, and ye shall receive the gift of the Holy Ghost."⁷

The interesting point here is the number of people that were baptized that day, for we are told, "Then they that gladly received his word were baptized: and the same day there were added unto them about three thousand souls."⁸ If a person only needs to accept Jesus as his personal Savior to be saved, then why did Peter and the other apostles go to the trouble of baptizing 3,000 people?

The *fifth* incident concerns the admonition Jesus gave to his apostles. After Jesus was resurrected, he appeared to his apostles several times to train them for the work ahead. On his last visit, just before he ascended to heaven, he told them: "Go ye therefore, and teach all nations, *baptizing* them in the name of the Father, and of the Son, and of the Holy Ghost: teaching them to observe all things whatsoever I have commanded you: and, lo, I am with you alway, even unto the end of the world. Amen."⁹ Thus, almost the last concern expressed by the Savior

---

6. Acts 16:33-34
7. Acts 2:37-38
8. Acts 2:41
9. Matthew 28:19-20

was the necessity to baptize new converts in the name of the Father, and the Son, and the Holy Ghost.

What Is the Meaning of Baptism?

To best understand the meaning of baptism, it would be helpful to examine how baptisms were conducted during the time of Christ.

Baptism Is to Be Performed by Immersion

Evidence suggests that when converts were baptized, they were taken down into a deep stream or river and completely immersed. This would help to clarify why John baptized his converts in Ænon, near Salim, *because there was much water there.* [10] It would also explain why Paul emphasized the fact that when Philip baptized the eunuch they both went *down into the water and then came up out of the water.*[11] It provides more meaning concerning how Christ was baptized "Jesus, when he was baptized, *went up straightway out of the water."*[12] It would also illuminate why early Greek transcribers used the word *baptizo,* which means immersion, to explain the baptismal process rather than *rhantizo,* which means to sprinkle.[13]

Baptism Is Designed to Symbolize the Death, Burial, and Resurrection of Jesus Christ

Paul provided more insights into the meaning of baptism when he said, "Know ye not, that so many of us as were baptized into Jesus Christ were baptized into his death? Therefore we are buried with him by baptism into death: that like as Christ

---

10. See John 3:23
11. Acts 8:38
12. Matt. 3:16; Mark 1:10
13. Strong's Exhaustive Concordance of the Bible: Greek Dictionary of New Testament (Dugan Pub., Inc.), p. 18 (907), p. 63 (4472).

was raised up from the dead by the glory of the Father, even so we also should walk in newness of life. For if we have been planted together in the likeness of his death, we shall be also in the likeness of his resurrection: knowing this, that our old man is crucified with him, that the body of sin might be destroyed, that henceforth we should not serve sin."[14]

In the above scripture Paul compares baptism to the death, burial, and resurrection of Jesus Christ. How is baptism comparable to the death of Jesus Christ? As Christ was crucified, or put to death, the past sins (old man) of the person being baptized are crucified, or put to death.

How is baptism comparable to the burial of Jesus Christ? As Jesus was buried underground, a person being baptized is buried (or planted) under water.

How is baptism comparable to the resurrection of Jesus Christ? Paul says that, as Christ was raised up from the dead by the glory of the Father, even so those who are baptized should emerge from the water to walk in a newness of life. This helps us to understand why Jesus told Nicodemus: "Except a man be born of *water* and of the Spirit he cannot enter into the kingdom of God."[15]

What Does It Mean to Walk in a Newness of Life?

Paul tells us that we need to put on Christ.[16] To do this we must "put on the new man, which after God is created in righteousness and true holiness. Wherefore putting away lying, speak every man truth with his neighbour: for we are members one of another....Sin not: let not the sun go down upon your wrath: neither give place to the devil. Let him that stole steal

---

14. Romans 6:3–6
15. John 3:5
16. See Galatians 3:27

no more: but rather let him labour, working with his hands the thing which is good, that he may have to give to him that needeth.

"Let no corrupt communication proceed out of your mouth, but that which is good to the use of edifying, that it may minister grace unto the hearers....Let all bitterness, and wrath, and anger, and clamour, and evil speaking, be put away from you, with all malice: And be ye kind one to another, tenderhearted, forgiving one another, even as God for Christ's sake hath forgiven you."[17] Thus, to walk in a newness of life means to commit one's entire being to become a Christlike person by emulating the example Jesus provided.

Does Baptism Signify the Gate Through which One Must Pass to Enter the Narrow Way That Leads to Eternal Life?

In the gospel of Matthew we find this admonition: "Enter ye in at the strait gate...because strait is the gate, and narrow is the way, which leadeth unto life, and few there be that find it."[18]

What is the gate referenced in this scripture? On the surface, it appears that any one of these three–faith, repentance, or baptism–could be the gate. However, if one compares the gate mentioned in Matthew to the kind of gate that blocks a passageway through which people enter only after paying admission, then it becomes apparent that faith and repentance are simply the price of admission, and baptism is the actual gate through which we must pass.

---

17. Ephesians 4:24-32
18: Matthew 7:13-14

Is Baptism Designed As a Symbol to Convey the Sacred Nature of the Ordinance and to Obtain the Most Sincere Promise Possible to Obey the Covenants Taken?

From the information provided, it seems that baptism is performed as a symbol or ceremony to enlist individuals into the organization of God. Is this really that unusual? In essence, we do the same thing when we induct people into certain organizations here on earth. For example, when a person is inducted into the armed forces of the United States, certain requirements have to be met for the enlistment to be valid.

First, the oath of office is administered by an officer. Second, the oath taken is standard, and every word must be repeated back to the officer administering the ceremony. Third, the ceremony should take place in the presence of the flag of the United States. This makes the occasion special, and impresses upon the individual the covenant he has committed to uphold.

In short, the whole point of the ceremony is to impress upon the individual the importance of the commitment he has made and to obtain the most sincere promise possible to obey the laws of the covenant.

It is interesting to note what other nations do to obtain a dedicated commitment from its citizens to defend their country. For example, to be enlisted in the armed forces of Israel, new recruits are taken to the ancient fortification of Masada, where the Jewish Zealots committed suicide in A.D. 68 rather than surrender to the Roman army, to be given the oath of service.

Is It Necessary to Baptize Small Children?

As stated previously, one of the primary purposes of baptism is to wash away past sins so an individual can have a fresh start in life. However, Paul said, "Sin is not imputed where there is no law."[19] To put it another way, there is no sin if a child cannot comprehend the law. Therefore, children cannot be held accountable to the law until they are old enough to understand it.

But what about the original sin of Adam and Eve? Are not children still susceptible to the judgment pronounced upon our first parents because of what happened in the garden of Eden? Children do not fall under this condemnation of sin. Paul tells us that Jesus has atoned for the original sin of Adam, enabling the innocent and righteous to return to the kingdom of heaven:

"But now is Christ risen from the dead, and become the firstfruits of them that slept. For since by man came death, by man came also the resurrection of the dead. For as in Adam all must die, even so in Christ shall all be made alive. But every man in his own order: Christ the firstfruits; afterward they that are Christ's at his coming."[20]

In his letter to the Romans, Paul confirmed this statement by saying, "As by one man's (Adam's) disobedience many were made sinners, so by the obedience of one (Christ) shall many be made righteous."[21]

Thus, baptism for children under the age of accountability is not necessary, because they are simply too young to understand the ramifications of the law and also because the atonement of Jesus negated any residual effects pertaining to chil-

---

19. Romans 5:13
20. 1 Corinthians 15:20-23
21. Romans 5:19

dren from the original sin of Adam and Eve.

This helps to provide additional meaning to the words of Jesus, when he said, "Suffer the little children to come unto me, and forbid them not: for of such is the kingdom of God."[22]

Must One Possess Any Kind of Authority to Baptize?

Three days after Jesus Christ was crucified, he appeared to eleven of his apostles and showed them his hands and his side so they would know it was really he and not some impostor. He said, "As my Father hath sent me, even so send I you."[23] Then the scriptures record that he performed an interesting ceremony: "He breathed on them, and saith unto them... Whosoever sins ye remit, they are remitted unto them; and whose soever sins ye retain, they are retained."[24] Since baptism is an ordinance designed to remit sin, it appears that Christ had just empowered his disciples with the authority to conduct baptismal rites. Is this really what happened? If so, what is this power? Where does it come from? How does one receive it? And what is it called?

According to the epistle to the Hebrews, authority is bestowed when men are *ordained* (or empowered) to act in things pertaining to God.[25] Paul said that no man can take this authority upon himself unless he is called of God as was Aaron.[26] When Aaron (the older brother of Moses) was called, he was anointed and sanctified so he could officiate as a priest.[27]

When Moses ordained Joshua, he set him down before all the congregation and laid his hands upon him, and gave him a charge, as the Lord commanded.[28] The authority that Moses bestowed during this ordination was called the "priesthood."[29]

---

22. Mark 10:14
23. John 20:21
24. John 20:22-23
25. See Hebrews 5:1
26. See Heb. 5:4
27. See Ex. 40:12-13
28. See Num. 27:22-23
29. See Ex. 40:15

It was also conferred upon Aaron's sons,[30] and substantially the whole house of Levi who were between 30 and 50 years of age,[31] and it was to be passed down through all the generations of Israel.[32]

There were two different levels of priesthood. One level was called the priesthood after the order of Aaron, and the second level was called the priesthood after the order of Melchisedec.[33]

The priesthood of Aaron was also referred to as the Levitical priesthood, because it was administered through the tribe of Levi.[34] An individual officiating in the Levitical priesthood (after the order of Aaron) was limited in the duties he could perform to help perfect the followers of God.[35]

An individual officiating in the priesthood of Melchizedek was empowered to perform duties that could bring perfection and endless (eternal) life.[36] The higher priesthood was named in honor of Melchizedek, king of Salem (Jerusalem), who was a priest of the most high God and friend of Abraham.[37] Originally, individuals empowered to officiate in the priesthood of Melchizedek were called high priests.[38]

At the time of Christ, the tribe of Judah did not have a bonafied high priest.[39] This situation was corrected when Jesus Christ, of the tribe of Judah, was called of God and given the Melchizedek priesthood and thus qualified to officiate in this position on earth as well as in heaven.[40] Jesus bestowed this authority upon his apostles when he ordained them to act in things pertaining to God.[41]

---

30. See Ex.. 40:14-15
31. See Num. 3:3-6; 4:2-3
32. See Ex. 19:5-6:40:15; Num. 25:13
33. See Heb. 7:11
34. See Heb. 7:11; Num. 3:6-9; Joshua 18:7
35. See Heb. 7:11
36. See Heb. 7:11,15-16
37. See Gen. 14:18
38. See Heb. 5:1,10
39. See Heb. 7:14
40. See Heb. 7:12-16,5:5-10
41. See Luke 6:13,9:1; Mark 3:14; John 15:16

The apostles, in turn, selected others to do God's work and set them down and laid their hands on them just as Moses did when he ordained Joshua.[42] As a result of this, Luke reports, the number of disciples multiplied greatly and a great company of priests became obedient to the faith.[43]

Indications that other ministers were needed to further the Lord's work in the holy priesthood come from the writings of Peter.[44] The Revelation of John informs us that the priesthood will exist throughout all eternity. Those who have lived worthily, so their sins could be cleansed through the atonement of Jesus Christ, will continue on as his ministers in the priesthood in the realms to come.[45]

If Baptism Is a Requirement for Salvation, What Will Happen to People Who Have Died Without the Opportunity to Be Baptized?

Since Jesus taught that everyone must be baptized to be saved,[46] and since the scriptural definition of baptism means "to be buried in water," what happens to those individuals who are basically good people, but due to events beyond their control, *die* without having the opportunity to accept the Gospel of Jesus Christ and be baptized? If God is fair, would He not have made some allowance, so all mortality could comply with His commandment to be baptized?

My first thought was that there must be some form of water in the spirit prison to enable baptisms to be performed, because that is where individuals are sent who die without having heard the Gospel, and it is there they will have an opportunity to either accept or reject it.

---

42. See Num. 27:22-23
43. See Acts 6:6-7
44. See 1 Peter 1:1; 2:5,9
45. See Rev. 1:5-6
46. See Mark 16:16

However, Zechariah said it is possible for a person to get out of prison even though there is no water there: "By the blood of thy covenant (Gospel) *I have sent forth thy prisoner out of the pit wherein is not water.*"[47] What Zechariah seems to be saying is that, though there is no water in the pit (spirit prison), there is a provision built into the Gospel plan that allows for a person to accept the Gospel and still be released from the spirit prison, all in conformity with the teachings of Jesus that everyone must be baptized to be saved.

The question now becomes "What is the provision?" While explaining to his listeners that life does exist beyond the grave, Paul refers to an ordinance that was performed in those days, asking: *"Else what shall they do which are baptized for the dead, if the dead rise not at all? Why are they then baptized for the dead?"*[48] In other words, Paul is trying to convince his followers that life does continue after we die. To support this belief, he asks, If life does not continue, then why are we baptizing each other for the dead?

This means that, during the time of Paul, a person could accept the Gospel in the spirit prison and have his baptism vicariously accomplished for him by someone currently then living on earth. Some individuals believe that Paul was simply referring to a pagan practice. But why would Paul use a pagan practice to teach a gospel truth? In other words, it doesn't make sense to use a false concept to teach a true concept. If a person is trying to teach a gospel truth, it is essential that an accepted practice be used to verily that truth.

This is possibly one of those ordinances that will be done for the worthy during the thousand-year period of peace that

---

47. Zechariah 9:11
48. 1 Corinthians 15:29

will occur following the second coming of Jesus Christ.

In chapter 4 the concept of the triangle of affection was discussed. It was mentioned that this concept was included in God's great plan so as to bind as many as are willing, who are currently living on earth, in the bonds of love (charity) and service. It appears that baptism for the dead is just another concept built into God's divine plan to bond together those who have passed out of mortal life, with those who are still living on earth.

This information gives new meaning to the Lord's statement concerning the coming of Elijah: *"Behold, I [God] will send you Elijah the prophet before the coming of the great and dreadful day of the Lord: and he shall turn the heart of the fathers to the children, and the heart of the children to their fathers, lest I come and smite the earth with a curse."*[49]

What better way is there to turn the hearts of the fathers to the children, and the hearts of the children to their fathers, than by establishing a requirement that though people accept the Gospel in the spirit prison, they still must have someone currently living on earth accomplish the ordinance of baptism for them to be saved.

If Baptism is So Important, Why Was It Not Recorded in the Old Testament as Being Performed in Those Times? Or Was It?

There is information in the Old Testament to indicate that the ordinance of baptism was performed. As previously discussed, one of the primary purposes of baptism is to symboli-

---

49. Malachi 4:5-6

cally wash away one's sins.[50] There are several passages in the Old Testament where this exact terminology is used in reference to the removal of one's sins. In Isaiah we find the following: "Wash you, make you clean; put away the evil of your doings from before mine eyes; cease to do evil."[51] And from Psalms 51: "Wash me thoroughly from mine iniquity, and cleanse me from my sin."[52] Again, from Psalms 51: "Wash me, and I shall be whiter than snow."[53] Thus, it is evident that an act involving the use of water was used to symbolize the cleansing from sin. However, instead of using the word baptized, the Old Testament scribes used the word "wash" to represent the removal of sin or iniquity.

In sum, I found that baptism is so important that the last admonition Jesus gave to his disciples before ascending to heaven was to go forth and teach the Gospel to all nations and to baptize those individuals who were converted to the Gospel.

Baptism is required for the following reasons: (1) It is a symbol or ceremony to enlist converts into the organization of God. (2) It signifies the gate through which one must pass to enter the road that leads to eternal life. (3) It is to impress upon the convert the importance of the commitment one has made to obey the laws of God. (4) It symbolizes the death, burial, and resurrection of Jesus Christ. (5) It provides a remission of sins. (6) It simulates the process of being born again so the recipient (unencumbered by the remorse of past sins) can go forward in a newness of life to become a Christlike person by emulating the example Jesus provided.

When converts were baptized, they were taken to a deep stream or river, then baptized by being completely immersed

---

50. See Acts 22:16
51. Isaiah 1:16
52. Psalms 51:2
53. Psalms 51:7

in water. This was done in the name of the Father, and of the Son, and of the Holy Ghost.

A person could accept the Gospel in the spirit prison (after having passed from mortal life) and have his baptism vicariously accomplished for him by someone living on earth, thus enabling everyone to comply with the teachings of Jesus Christ that baptism is a requirement to be saved to enjoy eternal life.

It is not necessary for small children to be baptized, because sin is not imputed where there is no law. Since children cannot comprehend the law, they cannot be held accountable to the law until they are old enough to understand it, and the atonement of Jesus negated any residual effects pertaining to children from the original sin of Adam and Eve.

An individual must possess authority to baptize another person. Christ empowered his disciples with the authority to conduct baptismal rites; and this authority, called the priesthood, is bestowed when men are ordained to act in things pertaining to God.

And finally, it appears that the reason the word baptism was not recorded in the Old Testament is that the Old Testament scribes used the word "wash" to describe the act of removing sin or iniquity.

6

The Fourth Requirement to Qualify for Eternal Life

John the Apostle said that in order to be saved and live where God resides, we must believe in Jesus Christ. "God so loved the world, that he gave his only begotten Son, that *whosoever believeth in him should not perish, but have everlasting life.*"[1] But here *is* the stickler! Paul said that no man *can* believe that Jesus is the Christ but by the Holy Ghost! "Now concerning *spiritual gifts,* brethren, I would not have you ignorant. *No man can say that Jesus is the Lord, but by the Holy Ghost.*"[2]

If we can't return to where God resides unless we believe in Jesus Christ, and we can't believe Jesus is the Christ except by the Holy Ghost, it logically follows that we need to exam-

---

1. John 3:16
2. 1 Corinthians 12:1-3

ine the following questions: Who is the Holy Ghost? What role does the Holy Ghost play in the salvation of mankind? Are the biblical references to be understood literally?

Who Is the Holy Ghost?

Paul teaches that only those who are *led by the Spirit of God* can really lay claim as rightful heirs as the sons of God.[3] It is the Spirit of God that can help us know what we must do to achieve maximum progression through mortal life. But what is this Spirit of God?

When Jesus was baptized, Matthew records that John (the Baptist) saw *"the spirit of God descending like a dove,* and lighting upon him (Jesus)"[4] This really doesn't answer the question, but observe the terminology used by Luke when he recorded the same incident:: *"The Holy Ghost descended in* a bodily shape *like a dove* upon him [Jesus]."[5] Thus, we have Paul saying it was the Spirit of God, and Luke records that the Spirit of God is, in fact, the Holy Ghost. It is the Holy Ghost who has the responsibility to lead us back to the presence of God the Father.

Comments from Peter and Mark indicate that the Holy Ghost is a personage and a member of the Godhead, along with Jesus Christ and God the Father. Part of this information comes from the book of Acts, where we read that Peter chastised Ananias and his wife for lying about how much money they had received from some property they had sold. Peter said, "Ananias, *why hath Satan filled thine heart to lie to the Holy Ghost,* and to keep back part of the price of the land?...Thou

---

3. See Romans 8:14
4. Matthew 3:16
5. Luke 3:22

hast not lied unto men, but unto God."[6] Here Peter is saying that if a person lies to the Holy Ghost, he is lying to God.

Matthew confirmed this statement by telling how Jesus equates the Holy Ghost as being on the same level as himself and God the Father. Just before Jesus ascended into heaven, he told his apostles: "Go ye therefore, and teach all nations, baptizing them in the name of the Father, and of the Son, *and of the Holy Ghost."*[7]

In the gospel of John, the writer refers to the Holy Ghost as "he,"[8] thus indicating the Holy Ghost is an actual person. This is confirmed in Acts, where the message directing Barnabas and Saul where to travel to preach the word of God is attributed to a person, that person being the Holy Ghost.[9] If the Holy Ghost is a person and member of the Godhead along with Jesus Christ and God the Father, what is his mission? What does he do?

The Holy Ghost Testifies That Jesus Is the Christ

John records that just before Jesus was arrested, he told his disciples: *"The Comforter, which* is *the Holy Ghost...even the spirit of truth, which proceedeth from the Father, he shall testify of me."*[10] It is apparent from this passage that one of the main missions of the Holy Ghost (Spirit of Truth) is to testify, or bear witness, that Jesus is the Christ.

If the Holy Ghost did not do his job, what difference would it make? If the Holy Ghost did not testify that Jesus is the Christ, then how could we believe in Jesus Christ? And if we did not believe, would we be inclined to follow his commandments?

---

6. Acts 5:3-4
7. Matthew 28:19-20
8. John 14:26; 15:26
9. See Acts 13:2-4
10. John 14:26; 15:26

And since Jesus said that he does only what his Father in Heaven commanded him to do,[11] it only stands to reason that we, in turn, would not follow the commandments of our Father in Heaven. Thus, we would not be doing those things that would develop our character so we could become like God the Father.

The Holy Ghost Bears Witness With Our Spirit That We are Children of God

Paul taught that the Holy Ghost bears *"witness with our spirit, that we are the children of God: and if children, then heirs; heirs of God, and joint-heirs with Christ; if so be that we suffer with him, that we may be also glorified together."*[12]

This corresponds with other scriptures that teach that there is a heavenly *spirit* family, that God is the Father of that family, and we are all members of this family: "For this cause I bow my knees unto the Father of our Lord Jesus Christ, *of whom the whole family in heaven and earth* is *named."*[13] Jesus said: *"The Son can* do *nothing of himself but what he seeth the Father do;* for what things soever he [the Father] doeth, these also doeth the Son likewise."[14] Again, Jesus says: *"My Father and your Father; and... my God, and your God."*[15]

Paul adds: *"We are also his [God's] offspring."*[16] "Furthermore we have had fathers of our flesh which corrected us, and we gave them reverence: *shall we not much rather* be in *subjection unto the Father of spirits, and live?"*[17] From the

---

11. See John 12:49-50
12. Romans 8:16-17
13. Ephesians 3:14-15
14. John 5:19
15. John 20:17
16. Acts 17:28-29
17. Hebrews 12:9

Old Testament comes this statement: *"Ye are the sons of the living God."*[18]

Can there be any doubt that there is a spirit family in heaven, with God as the Father of all spirits? Thus it is part of the mission of the Holy Ghost to bear *"witness with our spirit that we are the children of God:* and if children, then heirs; heirs of God, and joint-heirs with Christ."[19]

How important is it to know that we are spirit children of God? Several years ago an educational study was conducted wherein a group of grade school students were given an IQ examination. After the exam, the students were separated into two sections, with each section containing an equal number of individuals with the same intelligence score.

Though the students in both sections were of equal intelligence, the students and teachers of one group were told they had achieved superior ratings. Throughout the remainder of the experiment, this particular group of students were treated as gifted students.

At the end of the experiment all students were again tested. Those individuals treated as superior students had (as a group) actually rated higher on the second test than their counterparts who were treated as normal students.

What this study pointed out is that many individuals tend to limit themselves if they don't believe they can accomplish a certain task. On the other hand, if they believe they can do it, then the chances are greater that they will try and eventually succeed.

This appears to be the point Paul was trying to make when he said that one of the main functions of the Holy Ghost is to

---

18. Hosea 1:10
19. Romans 8:16-17

bear witness to us that we are the spirit sons and daughters of God. If we know we are children of God, then we would be more inclined to obey the whisperings of the Holy Ghost in order to become like our Father in Heaven and eventually joint-heirs with Christ in the kingdom of our Father.

The Holy Ghost Can Guide Us Into All Truth

The disciple John explains that another name for the Holy Ghost is the Spirit of truth, because *his job is to guide us into all truth.*[20] How is this accomplished?

In 1 Corinthians Paul explains that the Holy Ghost communicates directly with our spiritual conscience by bringing all things necessary for our spiritual and character growth to our attention and remembrance. These are the words of Paul: *"The Holy Ghost teacheth; comparing spiritual things with spiritual. But the natural man receiveth not the things of the Spirit of God: for they are foolishness unto him: neither can he know them, because they are spiritually discerned."*[21]

What Paul is saying here is that the Holy Ghost communicates directly with our spiritual conscience, and only those of us willing to listen and obey the whisperings of our conscience can be instructed in the things pertaining to God.

In Galatians Paul said that if we listen to the promptings of the Holy Ghost and do the things he tells us to do, we will walk in the spirit And if we walk in the spirit, we will develop those qualities such as, love, joy, goodness, etc., that will help us to inherit the kingdom of God.

Paul said: "The flesh lusteth against the Spirit, and the Spirit against the flesh: and these are contrary the one to the

---
20. See John 16:13
21.1 Corinthians 2:13-14

other: so that ye cannot do the things that ye would... *The works of the flesh...are these;* adultery, fornication, uncleanness, lasciviousness, idolatry, witchcraft, hatred, variance, emulations, wrath, strife, seditions, heresies, envyings, murders, drunkenness, revellings, and such like.. and... *they which do such things shall not inherit the kingdom of God. But the fruit of the Spirit is love, joy, peace, longsuffering, gentleness, goodness, faith, meekness, temperance....If we live in the Spirit, let us also walk in the Spirit."*[22]

Thus, Paul tells us that if we will listen to the promptings of the Holy Ghost and do the things he tells us to do we will walk in the spirit. And if we walk in the spirit we will develop righteous qualities.

The Holy Ghost Acts As a Witness in Things Pertaining to God When We Follow the Commandments of God

The writings of Paul inform us that the Holy Ghost acts as a witness to help us know the things of God when we follow the commandments of God: "We [the apostles] are his [God's] witnesses of these things; and so is also the Holy Ghost, whom God hath given to them that obey him."[23]

In short, it is apparent that the primary mission of the Holy Ghost is to be a testator. (1) He testifies to the truth that Jesus is the Christ. (2) He testifies that we are children of God. (3) He guides us to all truth. (4) He performs as a witness in things pertaining to God, but only to those who obey him. The bottom line is that the Holy Ghost performs much like a guide. He guides us to all truth.

---
22 Galatians 5:17-25
23. Acts 5:32

What Is the Gift of the Holy Ghost?

If these are the major responsibilities of the Holy Ghost, then what is the gift that Peter speaks of when he said, "Repent, and be baptized.. and ye *shall receive the gift of the Holy Ghost"?*[24]

Jesus answered this question while trying to comfort his disciples after informing them that he would soon be put to death: "The *Comforter, which is the Holy Ghost, whom the Father will send in my name, he shall teach you all things and bring all things to your remembrance, whatsoever I have said unto you."*[25]

From this passage it becomes apparent that the gift of the Holy Ghost can be interpreted to mean enjoying the companionship of the Holy Ghost as a personal guide to teach us and help us remember the things the Savior wants us to know.

Can a Person temporarily Receive the Gift of the Holy Ghost?

Luke tells us that on the day of Pentecost, when Peter was preaching to the multitude, they were *"pricked in their heart"*[26] by the Holy Ghost, causing them to ask, *"what shall we do? Then Peter said unto them, Repent, and be baptized every one of you in the name of Jesus Christ for the remission of sins, and ye shall receive the gift of the Holy Ghost."*[27]

An important point *to* note in this passage is that the multitude were pricked in their heart by the Holy Ghost to convince them of the truthfulness of Peter's words; but they could not receive the "gift of the Holy Ghost"[28] until after they had

---

24. Acts 2:38
25. John 14:26
26. See Acts 2:37
27. Acts 2:37-38
28. See Acts 2:38

been baptized. Thus, when the multitude were first prompted by the Holy Ghost, it was only on a temporary basis to convince them of the truth; however, to receive this gift on a permanent basis, they had to first be baptized.

How Does One Permanently Receive the Gift of the Holy Ghost?

Luke explains that the gift of the Holy Ghost was given by the laying on of hands following the ordinance of baptism: "And it came to pass, that, while Apollos was at Corinth, Paul having passed through the upper coasts came to Ephesus: and finding certain disciples, he said unto them, Have ye received the Holy Ghost since ye believed? And they said unto him, We have not so much as heard whether there be any Holy Ghost. And he said unto them, Unto what then were ye baptized? And they said, Unto John's baptism.

"Then said Paul, John verily baptized with the baptism of repentance, saying unto the people, that they should believe on him which should come after him, that is, on Christ Jesus. When they heard this, *they were baptized in the name of the Lord Jesus. And when Paul had laid his hands upon them, the Holy Ghost came on them;* and they spake with tongues, and prophesied."[29]

As Luke explains, the gift of the Holy Ghost is given by the laying on of hands following the ordinance of baptism. Thus, according to Paul, those who believe they can receive the gift of the Holy Ghost on a permanent basis any other way than explained above are harboring a serious misconception.

---

29. Acts 19:1-6

Who Can Bestow the Gift of the Holy Ghost?

As to who can bestow the gift of the Holy Ghost, an incident involving John the Baptist helps to answer this question. While he was in the process of baptizing some of his followers, he told them: *"There cometh one mightier than I after me, the latchet of whose shoes I am not worthy to stoop down and unloose. I indeed have baptized you with water: but he shall baptize you with the Holy Ghost."*[30]

This scripture indicates that John the Baptist only held the authority to baptize but did not have the authority to bestow the gift of the Holy Ghost, because he said someone would come later to fulfill this function. This information corresponds with the knowledge provided in chapter 5 concerning priesthood authority. If you recall, there are two types of priesthood authority necessary to act in things pertaining to God. The first type is after the order of Aaron, and the second is after the order of Melchizedek.

Information provided by Mark indicates that John the Baptist held only the priesthood after the order of Aaron, and thus could perform baptisms only for the remission of sin. It would take the Savior, who would hold the priesthood after the order of Melchizedek, (or someone he had ordained with this power) to bestow the gift of the Holy Ghost.

This explains Philip's actions while on a proselyting trip into Samaria: "Then Philip went down to the city of Samaria, and preached Christ unto them. *When they believed Philip preaching the things concerning the kingdom of God, and the name of Jesus Christ, they were baptized, both men and women....Now when the apostles which were at Jerusalem heard*

---

30. Mark 1:7-8

that Samaria had received the word of God, they sent unto them Peter and John: who, when they were come down prayed for them, that they might receive the Holy Ghost: ((for as yet he was fallen upon none of them: only they were baptized in the name of the Lord Jesus.) Then laid they their hands on them, and they received the Holy Ghost"[31]

So here we find that Philip could perform only the baptismal service. Since he did not have the authority to convey the gift of the Holy Ghost, it was necessary for Peter and John to travel to Samaria to accomplish this function.

Can Anyone Receive the Gift of the Holy Ghost?

The answer to this question is found in the story of Cornelius discussed in chapter 3. If you recall, Cornelius was an extremely righteous man, who did all he could to help the less fortunate. Because of his righteousness, Cornelius had earned the right to be accepted into the organization of Jesus Christ, but there was one problem. Cornelius was a gentile, and up until then the gospel had been preached only to the Jews. However, God sent an angel to Cornelius to instruct him to find a man called Peter.

In the meantime, to prepare the way, Peter was shown a vision. This vision was repeated three different times. In each case Peter was commanded by God to kill and eat certain animals that had previously been deemed unclean according to the Mosaic law. When Peter refused to eat the unclean animals, a voice told Peter the animals were not unclean if God had cleansed them.[32]

Peter did not understand the meaning of this vision until a

---
31. Acts 8:5-17
32. See Acts 10:14-15

short time later, when he met Cornelius. After exchanging accounts of their experiences, Peter knew that the gospel was no longer only for the Jewish people, but could now be taken to all believers in Christ.[33]

While Peter preached the gospel to Cornelius and his friends, the following occurred: "While *Peter yet spake these words, the Holy Ghost fell on all them which heard the word. And they of the circumcision [Jews] which believed were astonished, as* many *as* came with Peter, *because that on the Gentiles also was poured out the gift of the Holy Ghost.* Then answered Peter, *Can any man forbid water, that these should not be baptized, which have received the Holy Ghost as well as we? And he commanded them to be baptized in the name of the Lord."*[34]

From this incident it is apparent that though the Jews were first selected by God to receive the gift of the Holy Ghost, that privilege has now been passed on to all mankind. Paul confirms this by saying, *"By one Spirit are we all baptized into one body* [church], *whether we* be *Jews or Gentiles, whether we be bond or free; and have been all made to drink into one Spirit."*[35]

How Does One Understand and Interpret the Language of the Holy Ghost?

Before we can do the will of God, we need to understand the language of God so we can know what He would have us do. A person who has never learned German cannot expect to suddenly converse fluently in that language. It takes many

---

33. Acts 10:34-35
34. Acts 10:44-48
35. 1 Corinthians 12:13

months of hard work before the ability is finally achieved.

As learning a foreign language takes time and effort, the same may be said of the language of the Holy Ghost. The Lord said, "Behold, I stand at the door, and knock: *if any man hear my voice, and open the* door, I will come in to him, and will sup with him, and he with me."[36] Thus, if we are seriously trying to improve our lives, we need to take the Lord at his word and try to understand the communication process so we can know for ourselves whether the information presented in the scriptures is true.

How Does Communication Come from God?

Communication from God can come through dreams, visions, and angels, but the *normal* method of communication comes through our conscience in the form of feelings, urgings, promptings, and impressions. Since the latter method is the primary means God chooses to use, this, then, is the language we must learn in order to be conversant with God.

As mentioned previously, the conscience is the faculty by which distinctions are made between right and wrong in one's own conduct and character. In essence, our conscience is a mini internal-receiving system that gives us the ability to receive communication from the forces of both good and evil. When a situation occurs that requires a character-affecting decision, three factors combine to determine how we respond: (1) Communication from the adversary tempts us to make an evil decision. (2) Communication from God challenges us to make a righteous one. (3) We then combine the input from

---

36. Revelation 3:20

God, Satan, and ourselves, evaluate all three inputs through our conscience, then make the decision.

Through this method of communication, our free will is preserved in the following manner: Though we are tempted and challenged from opposite forces, we still make our own decisions. Thus, we still enjoy our freedom of choice and can select any course of action between the complete spectrum of good and evil.

What Roles Do God the Father, Jesus Christ, and the Holy Ghost Play Within the Communication Process?

Jesus Christ answered this question when he told us that the doctrine he speaks does not come from himself but comes from his Father in Heaven.[37] From this information, it is clear that in the beginning all doctrine originated from God the Father.

Jesus explained that following his crucifixion, it would be the responsibility of the Holy Ghost to relay these truths to us: "The Comforter, which is the Holy Ghost, whom the Father will send in my name, he shall teach you all things, and bring all things to your remembrance, *whatsoever I have said unto you.*"[38] From this it is clear that the Holy Ghost has been given the power to communicate to us the things that Jesus Christ would have us know that we might become even as he is in heart, in mind, in spirit in every way.

Another way to understand the relationship between God the Father, Jesus Christ, and the Holy Ghost, concerning the

---
37. John 7:16
38. John 14:26

communication process, is to compare the divine chain of command, consisting of the Father, the Son and the Holy Ghost, to the chain of command of a large corporation.

Many large corporate businesses are organized in the following manner. First is the chairman of the board. This individual is actually the head of the corporation. He normally has controlling interest in the company and sets the basic goals and policies concerning how the company is to operate. In short, he is the heart and soul of the corporation. He normally avoids the limelight and prefers to take the back seat by leaving the day-to-day operation of the company to the president of the corporation.

The corporation president is the second most powerful person in the corporation. He is normally hired by the chairman of the board and is given the responsibility to organize, direct, and control all corporate activities.

In a public service corporation, the relationship that exists between the public and the corporation is of utmost concern to the president. He is the head public relations officer and finances, organizes, directs, and controls the basic thrust of the public relations campaign. However, since this function is so critical to the corporation, the president normally has another individual assigned to assist him in reaching those individuals who are most likely to respond to what the corporation has to offer. The person assigned by the president to this position normally holds the title of Vice President for Public Relations, and is a key corporation executive.

As the head of His divine kingdom, our Father in Heaven occupies a position much like the chairman of the board. Since

Jesus Christ has been delegated all power and responsibility to organize, direct, and control all activities in order to carry out the will of his Father, he occupies a position similar to a corporation president. And, since the Holy Ghost has been assigned the responsibility to communicate to us, the information that Jesus Christ would have us know, he holds a position that is comparable to a corporate vice president for public relations. All together they form the Godhead, which, compared to a corporate chain of command, is similar to the key executive group that is commonly referred to as the corporate head.

What Did Jesus Mean When He Said That All Manner of Blasphemy Shall Be Forgiven Except Blasphemy Against the Holy Ghost?

Understanding that most communication from God comes to us through the power of the Holy Ghost helps us to comprehend a comment made by Jesus concerning blasphemy against the Holy Ghost: "Wherefore I say unto you, All manner of sin and blasphemy shall be forgiven unto men: but the blasphemy against the Holy Ghost shall not be forgiven unto men. And whosoever speaketh a word against the Son of man, it shall be forgiven him: but whosoever speaketh against the Holy Ghost, it shall not be forgiven him, neither in this world, neither in the world to come."[39]

This is a very strong statement for Jesus to make, because, seemingly, he places the Holy Ghost on a very important level. Jesus appears to be saying that forgiveness can be obtained when one speaks against him (the Christ), but woe to the man

---

39. Matthew 12:31

who speaks against the Holy Ghost.

Why would the Saviour make such a statement? John suggests that, possibly, the reason Jesus said this is because the Holy Ghost has been designated to act as our guide in choosing the paths we should follow. He also helps us to make correct decisions that will enable us return to the presence of our Father in Heaven.[40]

When we blaspheme or act contemptuously against the truths revealed by the Holy Ghost, we can end up losing the help he would like to give us, this is analogous to the person who is stranded in a pitch-black cavern and spurns the efforts of the guide who has been sent to help him to safety. Thus, when we blaspheme (malign) the Holy Ghost, we are, in essence, choosing to walk alone through the hazards of mortal life.

How Does the Holy Ghost Normally Communicate With Us?

To understand how the Holy Ghost normally communicates with us, there are three experiments one can try. These three experiments are extremely important, because when they are successfully accomplished, they can serve to teach a host of truths concerning how the Holy Ghost communicates with mankind.

The First Experiment

The first experiment consists of placing one's self in a state of mind where one can concentrate without being dis-

---

40. See John 16:13

tracted by any outside source. Once this is done, consult your conscience by asking, "What do I need to do to become a more righteous person?" Wait for the answer. It may take a minute or two, but you should receive an answer. You should not expect to hear an audible voice; however, you should receive a prompting, or an inner awareness, that will register in both your mind and heart, indicating what you need to do. Some refer to this as the whispering of the Holy Ghost, or the still, small voice.

This experiment is designed to show that the Holy Ghost can urge us to do something that will help us become a more righteous person. This will occur when we feel the initial prompting. This prompting will provide us with definite guidance to accomplish certain actions, and we will know exactly what we should do.

This experiment can also serve to demonstrate that, regardless of how much one is burdened down from the effects of sinful actions, the Lord is ready and willing to help, if we will just seek him with a sincere desire to change our current state of being for a better life. This will become apparent when, as we try this experiment and receive the initial prompting, we will feel a sense of awareness of exactly what we should do to improve our lives. When this occurs, it is God's personal revelation to us that He has not abandoned us.

When this experiment is successful, it can serve to illustrate that the Holy Ghost will speak to us on a personal level. We will know this, because his promptings will be tailor-made to what we need to do, not what our neighbor, relative, or close friend should do. For example, if a person is having a problem with alcohol, the prompting may be to solve this first, because only when this is surmounted can one be ready to accomplish more righteous works.

This experiment can provide us with an understanding of how simple communication from God really is! When we feel the initial prompting, it will take away the mystery surrounding how one generally receives revelation from God. Some individuals, when they become aware of this, are disappointed, because they feel that communication from God should be wrapped more in an aura of mysticism.

Another point this experiment can demonstrate is the necessity to set a reasonable pace in the quest for a better life. It is possible during this experiment to ask the Holy Ghost to know the first, second, and third most important things we need to do to become a more righteous person. However, this is not recommended. It is best to display obedience to the first prompting before asking for more direction.

In short, it is best to climb the mountain one step at a time. The speed with which we move up the narrow path isn't nearly as important as our resolve to just continue to make progress, and do so, at a pace that will allow us to reach our goal.

The Second Experiment

While the first experiment is designed to demonstrate that the Holy Ghost can tell us what to do, the second experiment is designed to show that the Holy Ghost can tell us what not to do. For this experiment, go to your Bible and open the Old Testament to Exodus, chapter 20, and read verses 3 through 17. Now go to the gospel of Matthew in the New Testament and read chapters 5, 6, and 7. Then thumb to chapter 22 and read verses 35 through 40. This reading assignment should take no more than ten to fifteen minutes, because it consists of only six pages. But take your time, so you can really ponder the message presented. Now select a day in the near future and make a covenant with yourself that on that day you will conduct all your activities in accordance with the information you gleaned from the reading assignment.

When the day selected arrives, if you will sincerely try to live that day in accordance with the doctrines you learned, then, whenever you encounter a situation where you are tempted to violate one of these teachings, you will receive a warning from the Holy Ghost. Once again, you will not hear an audible voice, but you will receive a distinct prompting, or inner awareness, that will register in both your mind and your heart that what you are about to do is wrong.

This experiment can demonstrate how the Holy Ghost speaks to our mind! When one completes the reading assignment, we are programming our mind with information about things the Lord has told us to do or not to do. After that, it is easy for the Holy Ghost to warn us when we are about to violate one of God's teachings.

When the Holy Ghost speaks to our mind, he speaks to our understanding. This is important to know, because it means that as we must learn math before we can do advanced calculus, in like manner, if we only have a first grade education in the Gospel, the Holy Ghost can only speak to us in first grade Gospel terms. Conversely, if we possess an advanced degree in the Gospel, he can speak to us in advanced degree Gospel terms.

The Lord gives us only that which we in our present capacity can understand and embrace. To communicate effectively with God, we need to prepare our minds. The Holy Ghost can (1) help us learn the principles God wants us to understand, (2) teach us what we need to do to apply those principles in our daily lives, and (3) bring to our remembrance where we stand in living according to those principles.

This experiment can illustrate how perfect our communication with the Holy Ghost really is! When we receive the warning of what not to do, we will know exactly what it is that we should not do. There is no chance for misunderstanding.

For two people to communicate effectively requires much more than one person speaking and another person listening. Effective communication is simply the accurate communication of a thought from one person to another. Though it sounds simple, in actuality it is rather complex. This is because our thoughts are influenced by a host of factors, such as (1) the way we perceive events, (2) what we think, (3) how we silently express ourselves, (4) our environmental conditioning, and (5) the native language we use to convey our ideas. The more mutual the understanding is in each of these areas, the more effective the communication is.

The Holy Ghost possesses the ability to read our thoughts. he already knows how we perceive events, he knows what we think, he knows how we silently express ourselves, he knows our individual environmental conditioning, and he speaks to us in a native language that we can understand. In sum, he understands us perfectly, and because of this has the ability to communicate with us in such a way that no miscommunication can possibly occur.

This helps us to understand how perfect our condemnation will be as we stand before the judgment bar of God after we pass beyond the confines of this earth life and try to justify why we failed to do the Lord's will during our sojourn on earth.

This experiment can help us understand why we normally do not recognize communications from the Holy Ghost. Some individuals, upon achieving success with this experiment, are surprised that they had not recognized the promptings of the Holy Ghost before, and wonder how they could have been so oblivious to his voice. The reason for this is simple. If someone begins speaking to us while we are concentrating on something else, it is difficult to hear what that person has to say. This occurs because our environment is filled with hundreds of different sounds, each of which has its own level of importance. To help us listen only to the most important sounds requires concentration. If we don't concentrate, we don't hear.

Our conscience operates on the same principle as our normal physical system of listening. It also requires concentration, and concentration requires work. If the Holy Ghost begins to speak to us while we are concentrating on something else, it is difficult to be aware of what he is saying. The reason most people are not aware that they can communicate with the Holy Ghost is because they have never made the effort to concentrate and put themselves in a position so they can become aware of his still, small voice.

This experiment can provide one with a testimony of how the adversary tries to countermand the efforts of the Holy Ghost.

When we try this experiment, as we receive a warning from the Holy Ghost, be aware of what may follow. Usually we can expect to receive an impression to disregard the prompting of the Holy Ghost.

This normally occurs because it appears that God must give equal opportunity to the adversary. When God allows Himself the privilege of warning us of a dangerous action to encourage righteousness, it seems He also allows the adversary to do the same to encourage wickedness.

Confirmation of this principle can be found in the book of Job where Satan is observed presenting himself before the Lord to express dissatisfaction for not being given an equal opportunity to coerce Job into forsaking his belief in God.[41]

It is important to know that the adversary possesses the same capability as God in his ability to communicate with us. He already knows how we perceive events, he knows how we silently express ourselves, he knows our individual environmental conditioning, and he speaks to us in a language that we can understand. He knows exactly when, where, and how to communicate his temptations so as to best achieve the most devastating effect.

This experiment can demonstrate what happens to our ability to receive communications from the Holy Ghost if we fail to listen and obey. As a test, when you receive a warning from the Holy Ghost, purposely do not obey it. You will normally receive another warning, only this time the warning will not be so strong. Eventually, if you do not act on the prompting, the warnings will get weaker and weaker then cease altogether.

What we can learn from this is that the Holy Ghost operates on the principle of use or lose. If we listen to the Holy Ghost and obey his voice, his transmissions become stronger,

---

41. See Job 1:9-12; 2:4-7

but if we disregard his warnings, his transmissions become weaker, and if we continue to disobey, we can lose contact altogether. When this happens, we lose the ability to discern between what is right and what is wrong.

Paul describes a group of individuals who had reached this state: "Having the *understanding darkened,* being alienated from the life of God through the ignorance that is in them, because of the blindness of their heart: who being past feeling have given themselves over unto lasciviousness, to work all uncleanness with greediness."[42]

Knowing that communication from the Holy Ghost operates on the use or lose principle helps us to comprehend how no man will be tested beyond his ability to withstand temptation. As Paul said, "God is faithful, who will not suffer you to be tempted above that ye are able; but will with the temptation also make a way to escape, that ye may be able to bear it."[43]

In essence, when we are initially warned by the Holy Ghost to avoid temptation, at that point we have the option to obey and withstand the temptation. On the other hand, as we disobey the promptings of the Holy Ghost and increasingly submit to the will of the adversary, we will gradually lose the ability to recognize communications from the Holy Ghost.

The Third Experiment

This experiment is designed to show what role the Holy Ghost plays when important issues arise in our lives and how the Lord wants us to gain the experience of deciding how to best resolve them. One of the major reasons we are on this

---

42. Ephesians 4:18-19
43. 1 Corinthians 10:13

earth is to learn how to make righteous decisions. If God were to step in and make every major decision for us, our ability to develop into a more righteous person would be destroyed.

It is extremely important that we have the opportunity to learn how to make righteous decisions. This experiment is designed to show how the Lord will encourage us to make right decisions and how the Holy Ghost can help when the situation warrants it.

For this experiment, select a problem pertaining to the spiritual and temporal welfare of you or your family. (1) Study the problem, (2) write it down, (3) list what appear to be the various solutions, (4) analyze each solution by listing the pros and cons, (5) select the solution you feel is the right answer, and (6) find an area that will afford some privacy, and kneel down and pray to our Father in Heaven, asking that if there is something seriously wrong that will affect your ability or the ability of your family to progress toward eternal life, the Lord will make it known so you can take the appropriate actions to best resolve the situation.

This experiment shows how the Holy Ghost can communicate so we not only know in our mind what He wants us to do, but we can feel it in our heart, as in the following true story.

A young woman needed to make a decision about a very important personal problem. She sought help from a friend who was receptive to counsel from the Holy Ghost. He explained that he could not help her, but that she herself should weigh the pros and cons, pray about the problem, then commit herself to a course of action. She followed his advice and within a short time found herself in a state of complete misery. She immediately took measures to reverse the action she had taken.

The next time she met her friend, she told him that the feeling of foreboding she had experienced was almost overwhelming and was most grateful that her prayers had been answered.

The experience of the young woman demonstrates that the Holy Ghost can stimulate feelings within us that serve to corroborate and emphasize his messages. He does this through both positive and negative feelings. An excellent example of the use of positive feelings is found in the gospel of Luke where an incident is described that occurred shortly after the crucifixion and resurrection of Jesus Christ.

The narrative opens with two disciples of Jesus on the road to Emmaus. After they had traveled some distance, they were joined by the resurrected Jesus, whom they did not recognize. As they traveled along, He expounded to them on scriptural references to himself in the scriptures.

When they arrived at their destination, they asked the Savior to have supper with them. Luke recorded that as they were eating, "their eyes were opened, and they knew him; and he vanished out of their sight. And they said one to another, *Did not our heart burn within us,* while he talked with us by the way, and while he opened to us the scriptures?"[44]

So here we have the Savior explaining the scriptures to his disciples and at the same time they were experiencing a feeling within their hearts bearing witness to the truthfulness of what was being said.

Lest we think events like this are recorded only in the New Testament, turn to Jeremiah 20:9, and we can read about

---

44. Luke 24:31

a similar event. Whenever we experience feelings of comfort following severe adversity, calmness in the midst of turmoil, acknowledgment of truth, feelings of love, comfort, joy, and peace of mind, be aware that we may be receiving communication from the Holy Ghost indicating that we are on the right track.

On the other hand, an example of giving in to a negative feeling is mentioned in 1 Timothy where it is stated: "Some shall depart from the faith, giving heed to seducing spirits, and doctrines of devils; speaking lies in hypocrisy; *having their conscience seared with a hot iron.*"[45]

Whenever we experience feelings of guilt, discomfort, shame, disappointment, disgust, premonition of danger, and the need to take urgent action, be aware that we may be receiving communication from the Holy Ghost indicating that we are on the wrong track and need to take action to correct the situation.

In sum, the Holy Ghost can stimulate any feeling, both positive or negative, that serves to help convey the message God wants us to receive.

If the Holy Ghost Is So Important, Why Is There No Mention of Him in the Old Testament? Or Is There?

As previously mentioned, by comparing the comments from Matthew and Luke concerning the baptism of Jesus Christ, we can determine that the term *Holy Ghost* and *Spirit of God* have the same meaning.[46]

Here are just a few of the passages in the Old Testament that refer to the Spirit of God. "The *Spirit of* God moved upon

---
45. 1 Timothy 4:1-2
46. See Matthew 3:16; Luke 3:22

the face of the waters."[47] "Can we find such a one as this is, a man in whom the *Spirit of God* is?"[48] "I (Lord) have filled him with the *spirit of God.*"[49] "The *Spirit of God* came upon Zechariah."[50] "The *Spirit of the* Lord God is upon me."[51] "The Spirit *of the* Lord caused him to rest."[52]

Luke mentions that when a person is filled with the Holy Ghost, he is able to prophesy.[53] This same ability is mentioned in the Old Testament in reference to those touched by the Spirit of the Lord. *"When the spirit rested upon them, they prophesied,* and did not cease."[54] "The *spirit of the Lord will come upon thee, and thou shalt prophesy."*[55] The Holy Ghost was known to Old Testament peoples; however, instead of being called the Holy Ghost, he was called the Spirit of God, Spirit of the Lord, Holy Spirit, or just plain Spirit.

Thus, from the information presented we can see the critical role the Holy Ghost plays in converting the natural man within each of us into the kind of person God wants us to be.

This role can be compared to the process used to refine steel. As iron is forged into steel by the hammer, the natural man is forged into a more noble child of God by the tutelage of the Holy Ghost and the trials and tribulations of everyday living. And as refined steel, with its imperfections removed, exists in a state of purity and strength ready to be put to use for the good of mankind, a refined child of God, with all imperfections removed, exists in a state of purity and strength ready to be put to use in the expansion of God's kingdom.

The following incident provides an excellent example of what can happen when a person has developed an ability to converse in the language of the Holy Ghost.

---

47. Genesis 1:2
48. Genesis 41:38
49. Exodus 31:3
50. 2 Chronicles 24:20
51. Isaiah 61:1
52. Isaiah 63:14
53. See Luke 1:67
54. Numbers 11:35
55. See 1 Samuel 10:6

A young man was relaxing after work one day, when suddenly he felt the impression that a good friend was in trouble and in dire need of immediate assistance. Most individuals would dismiss this prompting without a second thought, but not this person. Recognizing this prompting as something he had felt and validated through obedience to the spirit many times before, he immediately set out to find his friend.

After some time the friend was located. He was found to be suffering from a bout of severe depression and on the brink of taking his own life. The necessary help was provided, and today the individual who came so close to taking his own life is well on the road to recovery and most grateful for a loving and caring God and a dear friend who had trained himself to understand and respond to communication from the Holy Ghost.

In summary, the Holy Ghost is a personage and a member of the Godhead, along with Jesus Christ and God the Father. The purpose of the Holy Ghost is to (1) testify that Jesus is the Christ, (2) bear witness to us that we are the spirit sons and daughters of God the Father, (3) guide us in all truth, and (4) act as a witness in things pertaining to God, when we follow the commandments of God.

The Gift of the Holy Ghost can be interpreted to mean enjoying the companionship of the Holy Ghost as a personal guide to teach us the things the Savior wants us to know. This gift can be received on a temporary basis; however, to obtain it on a permanent basis requires that it be given by the laying on of hands following the ordinance of baptism. To bestow the Holy Ghost requires that the bestower hold the priesthood after the order of Melchizedek. Though the Jews were first selected by God to receive the gift of the Holy Ghost, the privilege has now been extended to all mankind.

The Holy Ghost can communicate to us through dreams, visions, and angels, but the normal method of communication comes through our conscience in the forms of feelings, urgings, promptings, and impressions. When the Holy Ghost speaks to our mind, he speaks to our understanding. If we have only a first grade education in the Gospel, the Holy Ghost can speak to us only in first grade Gospel terms. If we possess an advanced degree in the Gospel, he can speak to us in advanced degree Gospel terms. He gives us only that which we in our present capacity can understand and embrace.

The reason most people are not aware that they can communicate with the Holy Ghost is that they have never made the effort to concentrate and put themselves in a position so they can become aware of his still, small voice. The Holy Ghost operates on the use or lose principle. If we listen to the Holy Ghost and obey his voice, his transmissions become stronger, but if we disregard his warnings, his transmissions become weaker, and if we continue to disobey, we can lose contact altogether.

Jesus said that all manner of blasphemy shall be forgiven except blasphemy against the Holy Ghost. This is because the Holy Ghost has been designated to act as our guide in making decisions so we can return to our Heavenly Father. When we act contemptuously against the Holy Ghost we are, in essence, forsaking the services of the chief guide who can help us navigate the hazards of earth life.

7

The Fifth Requirement
to Qualify for Eternal Life

Christ told his disciples that they must be willing to endure to the end. *"He that endureth to the end, the same shall be* saved."[1] But what shall we endure to the end? James gave this answer: *"Blessed is the man that endureth tempta*tion: for when he is tried, he shall receive the crown of life, which the Lord hath promised to them that love him."[2] Thus, it is giving in to temptation that we must forsake, and endure to the end.

Is it possible to just profess faith in Jesus Christ and accept his atoning sacrifice and at that moment be saved? And

---

1. Matthew 10:22
2. James 1:12

once saved, does it mean that one can never lose salvation by yielding to the temptations of the adversary?

This is important, because if the "once saved always saved concept" is not valid, we need to know now while we still have an opportunity to do something about it.

To find the answer, we need to examine the following questions: Can one who has accepted Jesus Christ as his or her personal Savior fall away from the fold? and if it is possible to lose our salvation, how can it happen? what can we do? and how does the Lord help?

Is It Possible for One Who Has Received the Gift of the Holy Ghost to lose His Faith and Fall From Grace?

Paul taught: *"It is impossible for those who were once enlightened,* and *have tasted of the heavenly gift, and were made partakers of the Holy Ghost, and have tasted the good word of God, and the powers of the world to come, if they shall fall away, to renew them again unto repentance; seeing they crucify to themselves the Son of god afresh, and put him to an open shame."*[3] Paul *tells us* that, even though we are saved *by* grace, it is possible *to* fall from that grace if we become entangled *again in* the bondage of disobedience *to* the word of God.

In Galatians we read: "Stand fast therefore in the liberty wherewith Christ hath made us free, and be not entangled again with the yoke of bondage....Christ is become of no effect unto

---

3. Hebrews 6:4-6

you, whosoever of you are justified by the law; *ye are fallen from grace.*"[4]

How Can We lose Our Faith and Fall From Grace?

Our salvation is dependent upon our faith.[5] To have a strong faith, we need help from the Holy Ghost.[6] To have his companionship, we need to obey his guidance.[7] *We build faith by doing;* conversely, *we lose* faith *by not doing. If we lose faith by not doing,* it follows that *we can fall from grace by not doing* the *will* of God. Paul confirms *this* point by *stating* that though Jesus sacrificed his life so we could be forgiven of our sins, "if we *sin* willfully *after that* we have received the knowledge of the truth, *there remaineth no more sacrifice for sins,* but a certain fearful looking for of judgment and fiery indignation."[8]

What Keeps Us From Doing the Will of God?

The adversary is constantly parading his temptations before our eyes. Many of Satan's wares, when sampled, can provide immediate and temporary pleasure. Conversely, many of the spiritual blessings offered by God are normally not given until they are earned, and this can take time. In some cases, the more important blessings will never be received until we pass beyond the veil.

Many of us evaluate what the adversary has to offer as opposed to gifts of God and being greatly tempted by what we see and are simply looking for a good excuse to break down and sample the offer. When this happens, we normally try to justify our actions through the process of rationalization.

---

4. Galatians 5:1-4
5. See Ephesians 2:8
6. See 1 Corinthians 12:1-3
7. Galatians 5:15-25
8. See Hebrews 10:26-27

The Rationalization Trap

When some of us choose to abandon God and rely strictly upon ourselves, we become vulnerable in Satan's game of death. This is the reaction Satan has been waiting for, because it provides him with the opportunity to entice us into his kingdom of darkness.

When we enter the world of Satan, various temptations are provided almost immediately, for the quicker we partake, the sooner the trap can be sprung. The reason Satan acts so quickly is that when we become entangled in sin it is very difficult for us to do the will of God, because we don't want to feel like a hypocrite.

The descent normally starts out slowly then gradually picks up momentum as spiritual inhibitions crumble. As the descent continues, it becomes very difficult for us to stop. As we descend into darkness, the light of faith is gradually left behind until eventually all light disappears. When all faith is gone, there is no hope; and when hope is gone, there is no reason to remain righteous.

Deceptions the Adversary Uses to Encourage Us to Rationalize Our Lives Away

To encourage us to enter his rationalization trap, the adversary uses a variety of deceptions. Below are listed seven of the more insidious ones that we should be aware of.

The "It's Too Late" Deception

One of the greatest deceptions the adversary would like

us to believe is that, once we begin the descent into his kingdom, at that moment we have passed the point of no return; therefore, we might as well enjoy all his temptations, because all is already lost. Satan wants to drag us down to wallow in the quicksand of despair. He is hoping that eventually we will give up and commit suicide.

The truth is that, as long as we are alive, we can turn our lives around. An example of someone turning his life around is found in the story of David and Bathsheba. Though David committed adultery with Bathsheba and had Uriah killed, he was able to repent to the extent that he received a promise from the Lord that his soul would not be left in hell.[9]

The "You Can Always Do It Later" Deception

Another great deception of the adversary is that there is no hurry to change the direction of our lives. He wants us to believe that we can wait until the last minute to repent, and all will be well. The Emperor Constantine (A.D. 272-337) is an example of someone who was seduced by this lie. He purposely delayed baptism until just before he knew he was going to die, hoping to be cleansed by it from the many sins of his violent life.

The adversary wants us to believe that when God forgives us of our sins, at that moment we have qualified for eternal life. This is not true. Forgiveness just allows us to remove the weight of sin off our shoulders so that we can begin the process of progression. In short, it is what we do after we repent that counts. The longer we wait to turn our lives around, the fewer blessings we can expect to receive after we pass beyond

---
9. Acts 2:25-31

the realm of this mortal life.

Could we really expect a just God to do anything else? How fair would it be for a student to waste away a semester doing "F" work, then, suddenly, just before the end of the term, turn in a couple of assignments and receive an "A" for the class?

Jesus warns us to beware of this type of thinking. He taught that blessed is the servant who is found *doing* when he meets his maker, for God will make him ruler over all that he has.[10] In contrast to this, Jesus also said that the servant who knew the Lord's will and prepared not himself nor did according to God's will shall be punished and will be appointed his portion with the unbelievers.[11]

The "You're Doing Just Fine" Deception

This deception caters to the honorable men and women of the earth who lead a fairly ethical life but see no need to do the will of God to gain a valiant testimony of the Lord's work.

The adversary wants those of us who fall into this category to reason that the blessings we enjoy are really a result of our own abilities and that God plays very little, if any, role at all. Thus, we tend to become more concerned with achieving success in this life, and give very little thought to what needs to be achieved on earth to obtain success in the life to come.

Thus, as pawns of the adversary, we drift merrily along, very comfortable in our current state of being, having no desire to change our ways. If any thought is given to the life beyond, the adversary quickly steps in and tries to convince us

---

10. See Luke 12:43-44
11. See Luke 12:45-47

that, since we are leading a fairly good life, we will have no need to worry when the time comes for us to die, for all will be well.

Do the scriptures tell what will happen to those who follow this life style? Jesus taught that we stand a real chance of never being able to inherit eternal life and return to the presence of the Father in Heaven.[12]

However, the harm we cause to ourselves is just the tip of the iceberg. The real damage is borne by our children, who, because of the lack of proper religious instruction, grow up without a complete foundation in the teachings of God. They miss the opportunity to enhance the spiritual side of their life, and this impacts on their posterity.

When proper religious instruction is not passed along to succeeding generations, then the information will become more and more diluted, until, eventually, spiritual extinction may occur.

The "Why Me?" or "Why Them?" Deception

When someone experiences an adverse situation or sees someone else going through a period of tribulation, the adversary wants them to blame God for causing it to happen, and urges them to use it as an excuse to cease to do the will of God.

For example, a husband loses his wife, or knows of someone else who lost his wife or a loved one in an automobile accident. The adversary tries to persuade the individual to blame the Lord and to reason that if God is all powerful and all knowing, then He could have prevented the accident. Since God did not intervene, it means He doesn't care, and if God doesn't care, then why should one follow His commandments?

---

12. See Revelation 3:15-16

What some fail to consider when responding to this type of deception is that, if we are on earth to have the opportunity to develop our character, then adversity plays a critical role. If God were to interfere every time an adverse situation was about to occur, it would defeat the whole purpose of our coming to earth.

The "Fallen Leader" Deception

There are instances when a minister, pastor, rabbi, bishop, or other type of spiritual leader succumbs to the enticements of the adversary. The adversary whispers to all who would listen that this is a good reason to turn away from the commandments of God because, if this spiritual leader did not possess the faith to do the will of God, then the teachings of God must not be true.

Those who respond to this deception fail to consider that spiritual leaders, because their fall can have such devastating impact, are targeted by the arrows of the adversary with greater vengeance than the average individual. The failure of a spiritual leader to live righteously does not mean the teachings of God are wrong. We need to develop our own personal testimony and not rely on the faith of someone else in our bid to fulfill the requirements necessary to return to our Father in Heaven.

The "'You Need a Rest" Deception

When individuals who have been fairly active in spiritual activities begin to sag under the demands of the calling, the adversary suggests that, if they could only take a long vacation from any religious activity, they would then be able to return to the harness with renewed vigor.

What we fail to consider, when responding to this deception, is that assistance from the Holy Ghost occurs only *after* we do the will of God. When we stop taking an active part in religious activities *for an excessive length of* time, then the Holy Ghost ceases to help us resist the temptations of the adversary. The longer we are away, the less we want to return to the fold.

The "You Can't Trust God" Deception

When help from God for a perceived need is not received as expected, a painful feeling of distrust and disappointment may ensue. The adversary tries to persuade us that God doesn't care enough to answer our prayers.

When we respond to this type of deception, we fail to consider that in many cases a parent will refuse a request from a child because satisfying the want would not be beneficial to the child; similarly, our Father in Heaven may decline to appease our desires if the request is not right when all factors are considered. Just because we did not receive the answer we expect does not mean God did not answer our prayers. The answer may have been simply no!

To Help Us Overcome the Deceptions of the Adversary, Christ Established an Ordinance Designed to Help Us Rededicate Our Lives to Living the Commandments of God

To obtain success in any endeavor, whether it be temporal or spiritual, we need to set goals. As we progress toward these goals, periodically we need to stop and take the time to ponder and access our position as to where we have been, where we are, where we want to go, and what changes we need to make to get there. If this process is continually repeated, and the correct changes made, then success will be assured.

When the founding fathers of Alcoholics Anonymous initially established their program (as described in chapter 4), they recognized the need to incorporate this truth into their Twelve Step process. If you recall, Steps 10 and 11 established the need for alcoholics to continue to take personal inventories and seek to improve their conscious contact with God through prayer and meditation. The purpose of this is to remind alcoholics that they are never cured, but always only one drink away from slipping off the straight and narrow path into the prison of an alcoholic hell.

To accomplish an effective daily inventory, each night they conduct a constructive mental review of all their actions that day. Then they pray and ask God how their actions measured up to what is expected, to know His will and for the strength to carry out the promptings received. Each morning they conduct a constructive mental review of what they need to accomplish that day. Then they pray that they be shown all through the day what their next step is to be, that they be given whatever they need to take care of such problems.

As the founding fathers of Alcoholics Anonymous recognized the need to incorporate this truth into their Twelve Step program, God recognized the need to incorporate this truth into His plan of salvation. Thus, He established an ordinance designed to periodically make us stop and take the time to ponder and access our spiritual growth—where we have been, where we are, where we want to go, and what changes we need to make to obtain the goal of eternal life.

What is this ordinance? The night before Jesus was crucified, while he was eating his last supper with his apostles, he took some bread, blessed it and broke it and gave it to his apostles to eat. He told them, "take, eat; this is my body. And he took the cup, and gave thanks, and gave it to them, saying, Drink ye all of it; for this is my blood of the new testament, which is shed for many for the remission of sins."[13]

This was the ordinance, but what did it signify? To make this ordinance more meaningful, God chose to symbolize the ordinance by binding it (like the baptismal ordinance) to the crucifixion of the Savior. The bread represents the body of Jesus that was broken (nailed to the cross), and the drink represents the blood of Christ (that was shed on the cross).

But what does it mean when one partakes of the bread and drink? Paul recorded Jesus' explanation: "This do in remembrance of me... Wherefore whosoever shall eat this bread, and drink this cup of the Lord, unworthily, shall be guilty of the body and blood of the Lord. But let a man examine himself, and so let him eat of that bread, and drink of that cup. For he that eateth and drinketh unworthily, eateth and drinketh damnation to himself."[14]

There are two parts to this ordinance. The first part explains to us that when we eat the bread and partake of the drink, we are to do it in remembrance of the body that was given and blood that was shed when Christ made the atoning sacrifice. The second part explains that when we eat the bread and par-

---
13. Matthew 26:26-28
14 .1 Corinthians 11:24-29

take of the drink we are to reflect upon our current life style and determine what changes need to be made so we can continue to progress toward eternal life. This is why Paul said, let a man examine himself so he doesn't eat and drink unworthily.

When participating in this ordinance we should examine ourselves to identify any sins we have committed and then forsake them and rededicate our lives to keeping the commandments of Jesus Christ and God the Father. How long are we to do it? Paul said we should do this in remembrance of the Lord until he comes the second time.[15] Several passages of scripture indicate this ordinance was practiced on a periodic basis after the Savior was crucified.[16]

What Does the Old Testament Say?

If the God who gave us the New Testament is the same God that gave us the Old Testament, then the teachings concerning the need to endure to the end should be the same. Is this the case? Does the Old Testament teach that a righteous person can fall from grace? Yes!

The prophet Ezekiel said, *"When the righteous turneth away from his righteousness, and committeth iniquity, and doeth according to all the abominations that the wicked man doeth, shall he live? All his righteousness that he hath done shall not be mentioned: in his trespass that he hath trespassed, and in his sin that he hath sinned, in them shall he die."*[17]

What does the Old Testament tell us we should do to turn our lives around? In Ecclesiastes we are told, "Let us hear the conclusion of the whole matter: *Fear God, and keep his com-*

---

15. See 1 Corinthians 11:26
16. See Acts 2:42; 20:7; 2:41-42
17. Ezekiel 18:24

mandments: for this is the whole duty of man. For *God shall bring* every work into judgment, with every secret thing, whether it be good, or whether it be evil."[18]

Does the Old Testament teach that we should not wait to turn our lives around? Yes! There is a passage in Ecclesiastes that tells us we should not procrastinate the day of our repentance, that we need to take advantage of this life to prepare for eternity, because there will come a time after we die when no labor can be performed.[19]

What does the Old Testament say will happen to those who procrastinate making the necessary changes in our lives? *"The sluggard [slothful] will not plow by reason of the cold; therefore shall he beg in harvest, and have nothing."*[20] If we are slothful in turning our lives around because it is not convenient, then we cannot expect to return to God and inherit eternal life.

Is there any indication the fathers of the Old Testament practiced a certain ritual to help them forsake sin and rededicate their lives to keeping God's commandments? Leviticus describes a type of sacrifice called a *sin offering.*[21] During this ritual an animal or fowl without blemish is offered as a sacrifice.[22] The purpose of these sin offerings is to help sinners forsake sin[23] and rededicate their lives to keeping God's commandments.[24]

Thus, in the Old Testament we have a commandment from God to periodically sacrifice the body of an animal by the shedding of blood to atone for the sins of the people, so they, in turn, could reexamine themselves, forsake their sins, and rededicate their lives to keeping God's commandments.

---

18. Ecclesiastes 12:13
19. See Ecclesiastes 9:10
20. Proverbs 20:4
21. See Leviticus 4; 5:1-3
22. See Leviticus 4:3-28; 5:1-7; 16:3,6,11,15-19; Exodus 30:10
23. See Leviticus 5:5,13
24: See Leviticus 20:22-24

In the New Testament we have the commandment from Jesus Christ to periodically partake of bread and drink in remembrance of the body he sacrificed and blood he shed to atone for our sins so we, in turn, can re-examine ourselves, forsake our sins, and rededicate our lives to keeping his commandments.

Summary

In summary, we have reviewed the great plan God the Father has designed to give each of us the opportunity to progress to the greatest extent we are willing to attain. We have also examined what the scriptures say will happen to us after we pass beyond this mortal life. We have discussed the following five requirements concerning what we must do to qualify ourselves to accept the gift of eternal life.

First, be humble enough to study and develop the necessary faith to believe that Jesus is the Christ.

Second, truly feel the godly sorrow required to repent of past transgressions and make the necessary changes to live the commandments given to us by God, our Father, and Jesus Christ.

Third, demonstrate love for the Father and the Son by being baptized in their names as a symbol of being cleansed from sin and covenant to obey all of their commandments.

Fourth, receive the Holy Ghost (Spirit of God) by the laying on of hands by one having authority and yield to the promptings of the Holy Ghost to obtain the knowledge that highlights our imperfections and points us toward the kingdom of God.

Finally, develop the ability to endure to the end, to repel the temptations from the adversary to sin. These are the essential steps that we must take to overcome the world. Jesus said, "To him that overcometh will I grant to sit with me in my throne, even as I also overcame, and am set down with my Father in his throne."[25]

Each of us has been given our own moment in time to do with as we please.[26] We can use this moment to submit ourselves to the enticements of the adversary, or spend it by doing the will of god. Those of us who fail to heed the warning and live our lives in search of whatever the world has to offer will someday, after we die, finally realize, as did Esau, that we traded a mess of pottage for a birthright—in this case, a birthright to eternal life. Do we really want to take such a risk? The choice is up to us.

The Symbol

A butterfly flutters around a large clump of nettles and soon settles on a leaf, pauses for a moment, then departs. During her momentary stay on the leaf she deposits a number of eggs. In about five days the eggs burst open and out come baby caterpillars. They are small, ugly, grayish creatures with shiny black heads, and covered with short, stiff bristles. Almost as soon as they are hatched, the baby caterpillars begin to feed.

In about four weeks they are full grown. Presently, one will creep under a leaf and slowly spin a cradle of silk, fixing it firmly to the leaf stalk, using a kind of sticky glue. In this cradle, or cocoon, the caterpillar is quietly resting while it is slowly changing from an ugly grub into a lovely butterfly.

---

25. Revelation 3:21
26. See John 9:4

The cocoon hangs from the leaf stalk for nearly two weeks then suddenly bursts open. But now, instead of a black, bristly-skinned caterpillar, a beautiful butterfly appears, clothed with soft, downy hair and four exquisite wings. A pair of long, delicate feelers grace the top of its head, and two big, round eyes have replaced the six little eyespots, because now that it flies about, the insect needs to see where it is going. The butterfly also has a long sucking tube. No longer will it feed on nettle leaves. For the rest of its life it will sip nectar from the flowers and drink dewdrops from the leaves.[27]

The butterfly is now a perfect insect. It has gone through all its magical changes and has reached the most wonderful time of its life.

Comparing the cycle of man to the butterfly involves some striking parallels. As the caterpillar existed before it entered its cocoon, mankind existed before being "Cocooned" here on earth. To continue our development required that we enter the cocoon of earth life, with all memory erased of any pre-earth existence and no absolute knowledge that life will continue after we die. As a metamorphosis, or change, occurs within the cocoon of the caterpillar, our metamorphosis occurs within this cocoon of earth life.

The change that occurs in this life is caused from the two elements of good and evil. Thus, we are now pitted against one another, nature, and ourselves in an environment designed to cause millions of decisions. By choosing good over evil we develop and perfect our character traits. Finally, as the once ugly caterpillar emerges from its cocoon as a lovely, perfect butterfly, free to fly wherever it pleases for the rest of its life,

---

27. See American Peoples Encyclopedia (New York, Grolier, Inc. Spencer Press, Inc. 1962).

we will emerge from the cocoon of earth life by being resurrected into a new life with a new, perfect, immortal body, free to enjoy what our Father in Heaven has prepared for us for the rest of eternity.

When God is teaching eternal truths, He normally has prepared some type of a symbol to emphasize the lesson He would like us to learn.

I would not be at all surprised to find the symbol of a butterfly engraved or painted somewhere within God's divine kingdom.